The Lost Message of the End Times

The Lost Message of the End Times

IAN MILLER

RESOURCE *Publications* • Eugene, Oregon

THE LOST MESSAGE OF THE END TIMES

Copyright © 2021 Ian Miller. All rights reserved. Except for brief quotations in critical publications or reviews, no part of this book may be reproduced in any manner without prior written permission from the publisher. Write: Permissions, Wipf and Stock Publishers, 199 W. 8th Ave., Suite 3, Eugene, OR 97401.

Resource Publications
An Imprint of Wipf and Stock Publishers
199 W. 8th Ave., Suite 3
Eugene, OR 97401

www.wipfandstock.com

PAPERBACK ISBN: 978-1-6667-0724-3
HARDCOVER ISBN: 978-1-6667-0725-0
EBOOK ISBN: 978-1-6667-0726-7

Unless otherwise indicated, all Scriptures are taken from the New King James Version®. Copyright © 1982 by Thomas Nelson. Used by permission. All rights reserved.

Scriptures marked NRSV are taken from the New Revised Standard Version Bible, copyright © 1989 the Division of Christian Education of the National Council of the churches of Christ in the United States of America. Used by permission. All rights reserved.

Illustrations by d4 creative (www.d4creative.com.au)

07/29/21

To all who look forward to his coming.

Contents

Acknowledgments		ix
Preface		
The End Times . . . Could we have got it all wrong?		xi
1	First Things First	1
2	Prophetic Colored Glasses	7
3	Signs of the Times	23
4	Uncovering the Apocalypse	47
5	The War of Armageddon	73
6	When Christ Rules the World	100
7	The Mark of the Beast	115
8	Prophetic Times	140
Conclusion		156
Glossary		159
Recommended Reading		161
Subject Index		163
Scripture Index		165

Acknowledgments

Dr. Barry Chant—theological review
Pr. Bill Vasilakis—pastoral review
Tony Morgan, Dave Dennis, Alan Bailey, Christine Miller—proof and lay review

PREFACE

The End Times... Could we have got it all wrong?

Friday, March 7, 1980; 7:30pm—Redcliffe, just north of Brisbane, Australia. Seated at a kitchen table in the home of a pastor of a small church, I found Christ. Well, to be honest, he found me. Up until then, my concept of God was that he was neither safe nor accepting, so I had done my best to fly under his radar. Thankfully, he loved me enough to pursue me until I could run no further. I stumbled into his outstretched arms and found more than I could ever imagine.

It was 1980. Australian Christianity was in the grip of a wave of popular preaching about the imminent return of Christ. The gravitational effect of the alignment of the planets in 1986 was going to blot out the sun and fulfil the prophecy of Joel 2:31, "The sun shall be turned into darkness and the moon into blood before the coming of the great and awesome day of the Lord." Antichrist had been identified within various social systems around the world—the White House, the Kremlin, and even the Vatican. With the global introduction of barcoding, many saw the mark of the Beast.[1] Bankcard had been introduced to the Australian financial community in the late seventies. With its triple-colored, lowercase *b* logo, it looked like three sixes superimposed over each other. 666. The cashless society of Revelation 13:17 was upon us.

---

1. Revelation 13:16–18.

We were poised for Jesus to come back. All the prophetic markers were set to green. Wars and rumors of war. Unrest in the Middle East. The rise of international communism. Armageddon was most assuredly just around the corner. Adding to the growing anticipation, countless thousands of believers believed that God himself had told them they would see Jesus' return within their lifetime.

But nothing came of it. The fabled One World Government did not rise. We did not descend into chaos and anarchy. And Jesus did not come back.

By the nineties, with the collapse of the Soviet Union and the toppling of the Berlin Wall, preachers began to question if they had somehow got it all wrong. The USSR had featured in all the prophetic literature of the previous decades, and now it was no more. Unless, of course, it had not collapsed, and it was all a conspiracy orchestrated by Antichrist!

As a result, many church leaders either stopped preaching about the Second Coming altogether or did not go beyond the basics. "Jesus will come back. We don't know when. Be ready." It avoided the controversies, but left Christians in general struggling to understand what Jesus had meant on the Mount of Olives when he spoke of the signs of the times.

The first Gulf War brought the Middle East back into focus, and everyone began to rethink their list of candidates for the unholy trinity—the Beast, the False Prophet, and the Antichrist. Maybe it had nothing to do with Russia. But the decade rolled on and still Jesus did not return.

The year 2000 approached. And with it, fears of the Y2K bug and the collapse of the technological world. If ever there was a prophetic moment for Jesus' return, this was it. The prophetic timeline was coming into focus. Adam lived four thousand years before Christ. We were now approaching two thousand years after Christ. Four thousand years plus two thousand years equals six thousand years. And the Apostle Peter had said that a day is like a thousand years.[2] Six thousand years—six days, mirroring the six days of cre-

---

2. 2 Peter 3:8.

ation! What would follow was surely to be the seventh day, the day of rest, the millennium.[3]

And yet, as the clock ticked over to the turn of the twenty-first century, the occasion was noted for its ordinariness. Nothing happened. Computers did not stop. Monetary systems did not implode. Power supplies remained stable. The whole world had been in fear for no reason.

9/11 came hot on its heels, however. This had to be it! Antichrist had at last revealed his hand. The shocking atrocity of that day in 2001, as the Pentagon in Washington DC was targeted and New York's Twin Towers collapsed before a disbelieving and horrified world, certainly had a profound political and social impact across the globe, but here we are nearly two decades later . . . and Jesus still has not returned.

We find ourselves once more in a tumultuous world. As I write, most countries are shut down under the paralyzing fear of a global pandemic. Recent political and social unrest in the United States, the country with the world's largest economy, has spawned a whole new search for global conspirators and the rise of international tyranny. For a younger generation, unaware of the ongoing historical cycle that I have described in the last few pages, it has birthed, once again, a flurry of investigation into Eschatology, the doctrine of the Second Coming.

Unknown by so many, we have been here before. That whole generation of believers who, back in the fifties, sixties, and seventies, had devotionally heard the Lord tell them they would live to see his return have mostly all died. Maybe, just maybe, we continually pick up the wrong end of the stick.

What are honest, devoted followers of Jesus supposed to do with all the confusion surrounding the Bible's teaching of the Second Coming? For many, I suspect they just gloss over those portions of Scripture in their devotional readings; add it to the list of the many questions they intend to ask Jesus when they finally stand before him. And yet, it is clearly an important part of the Biblical narrative.

---

3. Of course, Peter also said that a thousand years is like a day. No one has ever suggested on the basis of this that the millennium is only one day long. It shows how arbitrary we can be in making the Scripture fit our beliefs.

Even a casual reading of the New Testament shows that the apostles all lived their lives with a conscious awareness of Christ's return. It changed everything for them—how they lived, how they preached, how they engaged with society, how they embraced the future.

> You also be patient. Establish your hearts, for the coming of the Lord is at hand. (James 5:8)

> And now, little children, abide in Him, that when He appears, we may have confidence and not be ashamed before Him at His coming. (1 John 2:28)

> But this is what was spoken by the prophet Joel: *And it shall come to pass in the last days, says God, that I will pour out of My Spirit on all flesh; your sons and your daughters shall prophesy, your young men shall see visions, your old men shall dream dreams. And on My menservants and on My maidservants, I will pour out My Spirit in those days; and they shall prophesy.* (Acts 2:16–18)

> Little children, it is the last hour; and as you have heard that the Antichrist is coming, even now many antichrists have come, by which we know that it is the last hour. (1 John 2:18)

> And do this, knowing the time, that now it is high time to awake out of sleep; for now our salvation is nearer than when we first believed. (Romans 13:11)

> Let your gentleness be known to all men. The Lord is at hand. (Philippians 4:5)

You would think, given our generation's widespread belief concerning the plethora of prophecies they believe are unfulfilled, that the apostles should have known Jesus would not return in their day. There were so many prophecies back then that had clearly not taken place. Unless, of course, the apostles knew something we do not.

And here it is. A truth the apostles lived by. In his Word, God speaks of our Today, not our Tomorrow. We fight our battles and experience our victories Today! We follow his call Today. There is a message of hope for Tomorrow in the Bible, but that hope transforms the way we approach life Today! It is all about Today! The message of the Second Coming is essentially not about the future. Bible prophecy is all about the purpose of God that has been revealed in Christ and the salvation that he offers us through faith in him. Today!

That is not what we have been taught. And it has colored the way we read the Scriptures. So let me take you on a journey through the pages of the Bible, and together we will gain a fresh perspective, or perhaps I should say an old perspective, on what God has revealed to us concerning the return of Christ. A perspective the apostles had. A perspective Christ himself had and still has. It will change your Today and encourage you to step into a new Tomorrow.

One final word. Before we dive into this amazing, life-changing message of hope, I need to make you aware that there is a vocabulary peculiar to prophecy buffs, some of which I have not been able to avoid. As you read this book, should any of my terminology be unfamiliar, just turn to the glossary at the end. Hopefully, you will find your answer there.

1

First Things First

IF GOD WAS TO speak to us about the last days, what would he emphasize? For that matter, would he even want to tell us about the end? What purpose would it serve? Our answers to these questions reveal our underlying beliefs about the world and the solutions required to meet its many problems.

THE MESSIAH AND HIS KINGDOM

In the world that witnessed the First Coming of Christ, there was great anticipation for a soon appearance of the Messiah.[1] The Jews were looking for their promised King. Although the Old Testament—the Jewish Scriptures—did speak about the Messiah and his Kingdom, much of the people's expectations were informed by the Apocrypha.[2] These books were written in the centuries after the last of the Old Testament books and formed the basis of a lot of the popular beliefs prevalent in Jesus' day.

For the first century Jew, the apocryphal teachings concerning the Messiah inspired hopes for a glorious, future world kingdom,

---

1. *Messiah* is the Hebrew form of the Greek *Christos*—i.e., Christ. In both languages, it means *anointed one*—typically a king or priest.

2. The word *apocrypha* comes from the Greek verb *apokruptein*, meaning *to hide*. The word has generally come to be used of ancient non-canonical Jewish writings.

with Jerusalem as its capital. According to those writings, the Messiah would be the greatest of all Israel's kings—but he would be human, not divine. His kingdom would be a righteous kingdom, in that Judaism would be the foundation of its rule. And it would subdue all nations of the world![3]

This inspired first century Jews. They were a proud people—God's people. It was humiliating for them to be subject to Roman occupation[4] and for their country to have a puppet Idumean,[5] Herod, as king. To the north in Galilee were the Zealots, waging a kind of guerilla war against Rome and the Herods; in the south were their Judean counterparts, the Sicarii. They were militants, inspired by prophetic zeal for a new world order. Their hopes were nationalistic, political, and military. The times were ripe for the introduction of the Messiah of popular expectation.

Much of Jesus' early preaching sought to redress these false expectations.

> My Kingdom is not of this world. If My kingdom were of this world, My servants would fight, so that I should not be delivered to the Jews; but now My kingdom is not from here. (John 18:36)

---

3. The following quote from the apocryphal Psalms of Solomon, written half a century before Christ, is an excellent example of this nationalistic Messianic belief: "See, Lord, and raise up for them their king, the son of David, to rule over Israel, your servant, in the time which you choose. O God, undergird him with the strength to destroy the unrighteous rulers, to cleanse Jerusalem from gentiles who trample her to destruction . . . and he will bring together a holy people whom he will lead in righteousness . . . And he will cleanse Jerusalem to a sanctification as from the beginning so that nations will come from the ends of the earth to see his glory . . . And he will be a righteous king over them, taught by God. There will be no unrighteousness among them in his days, for all will be holy, and their king will be the Lord Messiah." (Psalms of Solomon 17:21–32. Quotation taken from *A New English Translation of the Septuagint,* ©2007 by the International Organisation for Septuagint and Cognate Studies, Inc. Used by permission of Oxford University Press. All rights reserved.)

4. And before that, they had been under the Greek Empire, and before that, the Persian Empire, and before that, the Babylonian Empire! And the Assyrian Empire, and the Egyptian Empire . . .

5. The Idumeans were the same people as the Old Testament Edomites, a people with a long history of conflict with Israel.

The Kingdom he rules over is a family of faith whose members wholeheartedly delight in doing God's will and are empowered to push back the effects of Adam's curse. Without Jesus' emphasis of this new vision of the Kingdom, people would have soon accepted him as the Messiah, which could have so easily precipitated an armed uprising against the Roman authorities![6]

As a leader, Jesus did not at all resemble the Jews' anticipated Messiah.[7] He made no overtly political assertions. He was notably silent on important social issues and he accepted Caesar's rule. Though historically there were to be radical social and political consequences of his gospel, they were not the focal point of his preaching ministry.

When Peter declared in Caesarea Philippi that Jesus was the promised Messiah, this marked the beginning of a major reappraisal of Peter's belief system, one that Jesus had not overtly spoken into.[8]

All this is more essential for us to understand than we realize. The Messianic Kingdom is not political or military! It never was! It never will be! The fundamental problem facing humanity is spiritual in nature, not political. A political savior cannot redeem the world! No form of legislation can get to the root problem of the human condition.

The disciples so misunderstood this, despite their dawning awareness that Jesus was indeed the Messiah, that at his crucifixion they saw their hopes of national redemption shatter.[9] Even after the resurrection, they still looked for a political revival.[10]

The same misunderstandings are largely held by the Christian community today. Our world's problems remain spiritual in nature. Christ is not going to set up a political kingdom. That is not where the answer lies. We need solutions that resolve the corruption of our hearts—solutions that only the gospel can provide, not a political kingdom.

---

6. John 6:15 gives a glimpse of the strong anti-Roman sympathies that Christ had to contend with.

7. Consider Nicodemus's confusion early in Jesus' ministry, John 3:2.

8. Matthew 16:13–17.

9. Luke 24:21.

10. Acts 1:6.

Christians around the world fail to comprehend this and miss the powerful reality that Jesus is King right now. His all-powerful, world-conquering Kingdom is here. Right now! We need not wait for a future rule of Christ; it is a present reality.

Let me put it simply: Jesus is not coming back to set up a political kingdom with him as its King! Bible prophecy does not point to a global bureaucracy with Jerusalem as its capital. Let us put that one to bed; it is not going to happen. By the time you finish this book, you will come to see that the Bible does not even begin to suggest that such an event will ever occur.

THE HEART OF PROPHECY

In one of the amazing visions that John recorded in the Revelation at the close of the first century, an angel declared, "These are the true sayings of God."[11] Thinking those words implied that John was speaking to God himself, he fell to the ground in worship. The angel's response is illuminating.

> See that you do not do that! I am your fellow servant, and of your brethren who have the testimony of Jesus. Worship God! For the testimony of Jesus is the spirit of prophecy. (Revelation 19:10)

The testimony of Jesus is the spirit of prophecy! That is a huge announcement and is essential for us to hear today, and it would be helpful for us to know what it means. So let us consider for a moment: if you could distil Christ's teachings, what would you conclude his testimony to be?

It is obvious, really. Repentance, holiness, righteousness, mercy, faith, forgiveness, hope, the Fatherhood of God, the Person of Christ, the friendship of the Spirit, the centrality of the cross and the resurrection, and love for God, our neighbors, our Christian brothers, and our enemies. That is the testimony of Jesus.

But pay attention to what the angel said—the testimony of Jesus is the spirit of prophecy! There is a spirit of prophecy, a heart

---

11. Revelation 19:9.

of prophecy. Any prophetic interpretation must point back to the testimony of Jesus, those central elements of his message. From that one simple declaration—the testimony of Jesus is the spirit of prophecy—we learn the purpose of prophecy; it is to proclaim Christ and the salvation and hope that he offers. True prophecy will always speak of this.

Can you feel the weight of that? Any teaching of the Second Coming that does not underline the essential elements of Christ's message of faith, hope, and love misses the point! Stop and ponder that for a moment. If you study an interpretation of prophecy that does not inspire you towards love for Christ, love for people, hope, and confident faith—it is not on target. Do not waste your time with it. If it engenders despair, fear, or guilt—which some teachings certainly do—throw it away; it is not profitable.

A friend of mine once attended a conference on the *Signs of the Times*. The next week, he said to me despondently, "You wonder if it's all worth it."

I asked him what he meant, and he went on to explain, "I mean, having kids and bringing them into the world just as Antichrist is about to take charge. You wonder if it's all worth it."

The same voice of despair could be uttered amid the social and environmental turmoil we find ourselves in today. I am writing this book to tell you it is most definitely worth it! The teaching at the conference my friend went to had promoted a fatalistic message of doom, fear, and global conspiracy. It sapped him of faith, expectation, joy, and purpose. It was not the spirit of prophecy. It was not the testimony of Jesus. It was wrong.

WHY DID GOD MAKE PROPHECY SO CONFUSING?

The simple truth is that God could have solved a lot of debates by presenting a clear teaching that could only be read one way. Every other major issue of faith is discussed in the Scripture in such a way that there is little room for debate. Salvation is found in Christ. There is no other name given under heaven by which we must be saved except the Name of Jesus. Salvation is by faith, not works. No one can come to the Father but by Jesus. These truths are unquestionable if we take the Bible as the standard for our faith.[12] But it is cryptic when it comes to the teaching of the end times.

Many of the relevant Bible passages can be read in more than one way. Why has God done this? Definitely not to keep us guessing, always on our toes, as I have heard some preach. God does not hold people in suspense, nor does he motivate us by making us uncertain. He is a God of confident hope!

I sometimes wonder that God has written ambiguously about the end times so that every generation can see themselves in it and so find a source of encouragement. If that is so, then it may well be that the process of us diligently searching the Scriptures and wrestling with him over this matter is more important to him than the outcome of what we finally end up believing!

Challenging thought! Process more important than outcome! Relationship more essential than doctrinal correctness! That might explain a lot of things . . .

If we find in the message of prophecy, a hope that present wrongs may soon be righted, we will go close to the heart of why it is written in a way that can be open to interpretation. It speaks to us in the twenty-first century, but it needed to speak as powerfully to the people of every previous century.

For Christians through the ages, prophecy is a challenge to persevere and not give up because in the end, even our sufferings have meaning. And for the non-Christian, it unequivocally declares that no one can be certain of tomorrow. Today is the day of salvation and peace with God is not something that can be put on hold.

The Apostle Paul, when writing to the Christians in Thessalonica, declared that the hope of Christ's return should lift our heads and hearts in the middle of great trials and suffering. When viewed through the lens of Christ's return, we learn that even death itself is not the end.

> Therefore comfort one another with these words.
>
> 1 THESSALONIANS 4:18

---

12. Refer to Acts 4:12; Ephesians 2:8–9; and John 14:6.

2

Prophetic Colored Glasses

I SUPPOSE ONE OF the most difficult things to come to terms with is that there are four recognized schools of eschatological interpretation, and they do not even closely resemble each other.[1] What few people are aware of, however, is that their respective frameworks are built upon underlying assumptions. Though Bible teachers and theologians make these assumptions thoughtfully, prayerfully, and with careful Biblical consideration, they arrive at different conclusions depending on the assumptions they ultimately make.

- The first assumption relates to the people of Israel; they feature in many Old Testament prophecies. Who exactly are they?
- The second assumption relates to the intended audience of the prophecies. Who do the prophecies speak to?

Let me say up front, adherents of all prophetic schools of interpretation find Biblical support for the way they answer these questions; the Scriptures do not offer a definitive answer. Once the assumptions are made, however, they effectively color our reading of prophetic writings. It is as if the Bible student dons a set of glasses that predetermines how he or she will view the Second Coming.

---

1. For an excellent overview of the four schools, I recommend Dr. Barry Chant's work, *The Return*, listed in the Recommended Reading at the end of this book.

Without recognizing this, a proponent of one school of interpretation will read the writings of another school and consider them ill thought-through and Biblically misinformed—all the while ignorant of the fact that they themselves read the Scriptures through colored lenses.

Before we go any further in our study of the end times, then, we need to look closely at these two key questions and see how the various schools of interpretation answer them. In that way, we will be able to determine which lens best underlines the centrality of the testimony of Jesus, the spirit of prophecy.

WHO IS THE ISRAEL OF BIBLE PROPHECY?

Many Old Testament prophecies relate directly to this people group, so it is important to determine who they are. You might think the answer is obvious, but did you know that the Bible identifies more than one group of people as Israel? Let me give you a bit of the historical background to the prophetic writings of the Old Testament.

When the Israelites left Egypt under the leadership of Moses, and later Joshua, they were a united group, known collectively by the name of their forefather, Israel. Centuries later, when the people crowned Saul as king over them, the kingdom of Israel was founded. Saul's dynasty was short-lived, however. The monarchy shifted to David and afterwards to his son, Solomon. When Solomon's son, Rehoboam, was crowned, political unrest was sparked, and the nation divided into two separate kingdoms. To the south was the nation known as Judah, with its capital in Jerusalem, and to the north was the nation called Israel, with its capital in Samaria. A couple of centuries later, the northern nation, Israel, was taken into captivity by the Assyrians. It ceased to be a political entity from that time on, its people having been dispersed across the lands of the Assyrian Empire, present day northern Iraq. A century later again, we find the southern nation of Judah in captivity under the Babylonians in the delta region of southern Iraq and Iran, near the Persian Gulf. Ezekiel, writing during this captivity, applied the name Israel to the nation of Judah.² By New Testament times, these same Jewish people were commonly known as the people of Israel.³ In the midst of this, the Apostle Paul metaphorically called the church, Israel.⁴

So, when the Old Testament refers prophetically to Israel in relation to the end times, who is it talking about? The collective united group of people? The people of the northern kingdom who, for the most part, were lost to history after the Assyrian deportation? The Jews of the southern kingdom? Or the church? The answer to that question has far reaching implications.

Dispensational premillennialists look for fulfilment within the modern Jewish state. Historical premillennialists see the promises being outworked in the lost people of the northern kingdom.⁵ Preterists consider the promises already fulfilled in the Jewish people of the ancient world. Idealists tend to see the promises as applying to the church.⁶

WHO WAS PROPHECY WRITTEN FOR?

The second assumption involves the intended audience of prophetic writings. Is prophecy only to be understood in terms of events that occur at the very end of the age, and so speaks to the generation that is alive at the time of Christ's return, as the Dispensationalist believes? That is, does Bible prophecy only speak of the end? Or, as the Historicist claims, does prophecy cover, in panoramic fashion, the unfolding history of God's dealings with humanity? Can we, today, find ourselves somewhere along God's prophetic timeline?

2. Ezekiel 3:1–7.
3. Luke 7:9; John 1:31; Romans 9:3–5.
4. Galatians 6:16.
5. This people group must be found historically, as the nation is not directly discussed, as a nation, in the Bible after the Assyrian deportation. Many theories have been put forward in identifying them. One common view, known as British Israelism, is that Anglo-Saxons are the progeny of the northern people of Israel. This is not the only theory, however. There is a belief that the peoples of the Indian subcontinent are the descendants of that northern kingdom.

6. This may not be rigidly adhered to as a consequence of the next assumption to be discussed.

On the other hand, did the prophecies relate specifically to the generation of the prophet? Was God speaking through the prophets about events and issues that were contemporary to the prophets? If that is the case, those prophecies have nothing to do with the return of Christ and we are looking for fulfilments that have already come and gone. Preterists see it that way. Finally, can there be more than one application of a prophetic announcement? The Idealist maintains that prophecy is relevant to any person or people who find themselves in similar situations to those depicted. They see cyclic repetitions of fulfilment to prophecy.

PUTTING ON THE GLASSES

As you can see, our responses to these fundamental questions generate huge differences in our interpretation of Bible prophecy. So what assumptions are the ones we should make? Allow me to help you.

We have already seen that the prophetic glasses we wear significantly influence our understanding. Keep in mind the important revelation that the testimony of Jesus is the spirit of prophecy. That is going to be our guiding principle. Our interpretation of prophecy needs to be one that underlines faith, hope, love, and the victory of God through Jesus' death and resurrection. It needs, therefore, to speak powerfully to all people in all generations. We will reject assumptions that lead to a message of fear or global doom. We will reject assumptions that lead to a view of prophecy that no one can understand unless they are students of history or global affairs. We will reject assumptions that lead to a view of prophecy that is irrelevant for the majority of Christians since the birth of the church.

So come with me. Let me guide you through the prophecy maze and arrive at a clear, easily understood, faith-inspiring, hope-filled, God-glorifying message of the return of Christ. One that will transform your Today and shape your Tomorrow. Our world is desperate for it.

> For the earnest expectation of the creation eagerly waits for the revealing of the sons of God. For the creation was subjected to futility, not willingly, but because of Him

who subjected it in hope; because the creation itself also will be delivered from the bondage of corruption into the glorious liberty of the children of God. For we know that the whole creation groans and labors with birth pangs together until now. (Romans 8:19–22)

OUR FIRST SET OF GLASSES—WHO IS ISRAEL?

In order to open this one up to you, I need to take you to the pages of the New Testament where the Apostle Paul speaks about the mystery of God.

> If indeed you have heard of the dispensation of the grace of God which was given to me for you, how that by revelation He made known to me the mystery (as I have briefly written already, by which, when you read, you may understand my knowledge in the mystery of Christ), which in other ages was not made known to the sons of men, as it has now been revealed by the Spirit to His holy apostles and prophets. (Ephesians 3:2–5)

The common English word, *mystery*, means a *puzzle*, one that can be solved if you are clever enough. But the word that appears in the New Testament means something very different. Not all the facts have been revealed! At the time Paul wrote his letter to the Ephesians, there was a host of what the Greeks called, mystery religions. These promoted beliefs and rites that only initiates had access to. Secret knowledge. Mysteries are hidden!

When Paul talks of the *mystery*, then, he is speaking of something that no one can know unless it is revealed to them. That is why he says the mystery had been made known to him by revelation. This mystery was there in the Old Testament, but it was hidden. But it has been revealed in the New Testament.

> And to make all see what is the fellowship of the mystery, which from the beginning of the ages has been hidden in God who created all things through Jesus Christ; to the intent that now the manifold wisdom of God might

be made known by the church to the principalities and powers in the heavenly places. (Ephesians 3:9–10)

So then, what is this mystery, this hidden secret of God?

> That the Gentiles should be fellow heirs, of the same body, and partakers of His promise in Christ through the gospel. (Ephesians 3:6)

The mystery is that, in the New Covenant, the Gentiles become identical in the eyes of God with Israel, the Old Covenant people of God. Earlier in Ephesians, Paul expressed that in the church there is no difference between Jew and Gentile—they are all fellow-citizens with God's people, members of his household.

> For He Himself is our peace, who has made both *(Jew and Gentile)* one, and has broken down the middle wall of separation, having abolished in His flesh the enmity, that is, the law of commandments contained in ordinances, so as to create in Himself one new man from the two *(Jew and Gentile)*, thus making peace, and that He might reconcile them both to God in one body through the cross, thereby putting to death the enmity. (Ephesians 2:14–16)

Reconciled to God in one body. That body is the church.

> And He put all things under His feet and gave Him to be head over all things to the church, which is His body, the fullness of Him who fills all in all. (Ephesians 1:22–23)

This is illustrated diagrammatically below.

Ephesians 2:11—3:11

```
        ┌──────────────────┐
        │  Under One Head  │
        └────────┬─────────┘
                 ▼
        ┌──────────────────┐
        │   One New Man    │
        └──────────────────┘
             ▲        ▲
┌──────────┐           ┌──────────┐
│  Israel  │ ◄──────── │ Gentiles │
└──────────┘           └──────────┘
```

Prophetic Colored Glasses

In the Old Testament, there was a declaration that the Gentiles would come into relationship with God.[7] However, there was no obvious reference to them becoming one with Israel, God's people. They could convert to the Jewish faith, but throughout the Old Testament there was always a marked distinction between the natural-born Jew and the Gentile convert.

However, the church—consisting equally of Jew and Gentile—is not easily seen in the Old Testament promises of the New Covenant. That is why the early apostles were amazed when God saved the Roman centurion, Cornelius, and his household, and filled them with his Spirit.[8] And they were not even circumcised Gentile converts to Judaism!

Paul said that this had been hidden from generations past. Jew and Gentile becoming one body in Christ is there in the Old Testament, but it is hidden, a mystery that needs a key to unlock it. When we read the Old Testament, then, we have to accept that within its pages is a hidden, New Testament, new creation church. But it is a mystery, one that you will not recognize unless you have been shown how to see it.

Some of you are thinking right now that it would have been helpful if Paul had demonstrated how the New Testament church was hidden in the Old Testament promises. In fact, with a little bit of study, we will find that he did. For this, let us go to a passage where Paul discussed the Old Testament prediction of the conversion of the Gentiles.

> As He says also in Hosea: "I will call them My people, who were not My people, and her beloved, who was not beloved." "And it shall come to pass in the place where it was said to them, 'You are not My people,' there they shall be called sons of the living God." (Romans 9:25–26)

Paul quoted from two passages—Hosea 2:23 and Hosea 1:10. Keeping in context with Romans 9, Paul was speaking in reference to the salvation of the Gentiles. It was certainly said of them, "They are not God's people," and they were definitely not his beloved. For

---

7. See for example Isaiah 11:10.
8. Acts 10:45; 11:18.

the most part, that is where many commentators and Bible students land, showing how the two descriptions apply to the Gentiles. But if we study those same verses within their contexts in Hosea, a stunning observation is made.

At the time of Hosea's writing, the Israelite people were divided. About two hundred years earlier, a civil revolt had resulted in the nation separating into two. As we learned earlier in this chapter, the southern kingdom was called Judah (Judea by New Testament times) after its principal tribe, and the northern kingdom was called Israel.[9]

Ever since its revolt against Judah, the northern kingdom of Israel had been a godless nation. The Lord had sent many prophets to warn them to repent, but to no avail. Hosea was one of these, declaring that judgment awaited them because of their unfaithfulness to YHWH,[10] their covenant making God. Within fifty years of his writing, Israel, the northern kingdom, was carried away into captivity by the Assyrians, never to be known of as a distinct nation again.

If we look closely at Hosea's message, however, we will see the Apostle Paul's hidden mystery.

---

9. Sometimes the northern kingdom was called Ephraim by the prophets, after its principal tribe.

10. Known as the Tetragrammaton, the four letters YHWH are the Hebrew rendering of the personal name of God used throughout the Old Testament. The most ancient Hebrew writings did not record vowel sounds, only consonants. Those who were familiar with Hebrew could easily include the vowels from their knowledge of the language. Unfortunately, probably originating from the time of the Babylonian captivity, Jewish speakers refrained from speaking the name of God. Quickly over time, then, the vowel sounds for the Tetragrammaton were forgotten. All that has come down to us are the consonants YHWH. A practice going back before the translation of the Bible into English was to insert the vowels e, o, and a between the four consonants. YeHoWaH, or in the old English, JeHoVaH. Scholarship of the twentieth century concluded that the vowel sounds were more likely a and e, forming the Name YaHWeH, the causative of the first person verb *to be*: "I cause to be." This relates strongly to God's declaration to Moses, "I am who I am." Whenever you see the word LORD in the Old Testament, using the Small Caps script (as opposed to the standard Lord, meaning Master), you are looking at the Hebrew name of God, YHWH, "I cause to be."

Prophetic Colored Glasses

Hosea 1:2–9 depicts the prophet being instructed by God to take a prostitute for his wife and of her giving birth to three children. The names given to them had special significance in relation to God's impending judgment on Israel.

> When the LORD began to speak by Hosea, the LORD said to Hosea, "Go, take yourself a wife of harlotry and children of harlotry, for the land has committed great harlotry by departing from the LORD." So he went and took Gomer the daughter of Diblaim, and she conceived and bore him a son. Then the LORD said to him: "Call his name Jezreel, for in a little while I will avenge the bloodshed of Jezreel on the house of Jehu, and bring an end to the kingdom of the house of Israel. It shall come to pass in that day that I will break the bow of Israel in the Valley of Jezreel." (Hosea 1:2–5)

In accordance with the LORD's instruction, Hosea married the prostitute as an illustration of God's betrothal to unfaithful Israel. A son was conceived. He was called Jezreel because God would judge the house of Jehu (one of the kings of the northern nation of Israel) for the massacre of Ahab's family at Jezreel.[11] And note particularly what God said in verses four and five concerning Israel: he would bring an end to the kingdom of the house of Israel and break the bow of Israel.

The narrative goes on.

> And she conceived again and bore a daughter. Then God said to him: "Call her name Lo-Ruhamah, for I will no longer have mercy on the house of Israel, but I will utterly take them away. Yet I will have mercy on the house of Judah, will save them by the LORD their God, and will not save them by bow, nor by sword or battle, by horses or horsemen." (Hosea 1:6–7)

In the Hebrew tongue, *Lo-Ruhamah* means *No Mercy*. The reason? Because God would no longer show mercy to the house of Israel, the northern kingdom. Yet, though he would not save Israel, he would show mercy to Judah and would save them.

---

11. See 2 Kings 10:11.

> Now when she had weaned Lo-Ruhamah, she conceived and bore a son. Then God said: "Call his name Lo-Ammi, for you are not My people, and I will not be your God." (Hosea 1:8–9)

Lo-Ammi is Hebrew for *Not My People*. You cannot get a clearer message than that! God did not recognize the northern kingdom of Israel as his people, and he was going to put an end to their kingdom, showing them no mercy or forgiveness. Before half a century had passed, Israel, the northern kingdom, was no more. Such is the power of God's judgment!

The verses that follow, however, are totally out of place.

> Yet the number of the children of Israel shall be as the sand of the sea, which cannot be measured or numbered. And it shall come to pass in the place where it was said to them, "You are not My people" *(you are Lo-Ammi)*, there it shall be said to them, "You are sons of the living God." Then the children of Judah and the children of Israel shall be gathered together and appoint for themselves one head; and they shall come up out of the land, for great will be the day of Jezreel. Say to your brethren, "My people," *(Ammi)* and to your sisters, "Mercy is shown." *(Ruhamah)* (Hosea 1:10–2:1)

The Israelites will be as numerous as the sand on the seashore! The people of Judah and the people of Israel will be reunited, and they will appoint one leader! Surely this stands in contradiction to the finality of the judgment on Israel that we have just studied!

To complicate matters further, Paul, in Romans, quoted this contradictory passage as referring to the conversion of the Gentiles, not Israel. His other quote comes from the end of chapter two.

> Then I will sow her *(Israel)* for Myself in the earth; and I will have mercy on her who had not obtained mercy *(Lo-Ruhamah)*; then I will say to those who were not My people *(Lo-Ammi)*, "You are My people!" and they shall say, "You are my God." (Hosea 2:23)

In keeping with Hosea's context, this is a classic contradiction to what the prophet had just said concerning Israel. God will no longer show mercy to the house of Israel (Hosea 1:6) but he will show them his mercy (Hosea 2:23)!

Keep in mind, however, that there is a mystery in the Old Testament. A hidden truth that Gentile and Jew come together to form the New Testament church. In that light, the contradiction of Hosea chapters one and two disappears and Paul's application of Hosea's prophecy to the Gentiles becomes clear.

Hosea 1:2-9 refers to the overthrow of the earthly, northern kingdom of Israel that took place some fifty years after Hosea's prophecy. The verses that followed refer, not to Israel, the Old Testament people of God, but to the Gentiles. They are a veiled reflection of the church. Paul saw in Hosea 1:10 a reference to the Gentiles entering salvation, a verse that spoke in terms of Israel!

> Then the children of Judah and the children of Israel shall be gathered together, and appoint for themselves one head; and they shall come up out of the land, for great will be the day of Jezreel! (Hosea 1:11)

With that understanding, we then see that Israel and Judah uniting under one head is Gentile and Jew becoming one body under the headship of Christ. It speaks prophetically and dramatically of the church!

This mirrors Paul's doctrine of the church that we have previously discussed from his letter to the Ephesians. In the diagram below, I have represented it in such a way as to show its similarity with our earlier diagram of Ephesians 2:11-3:11.

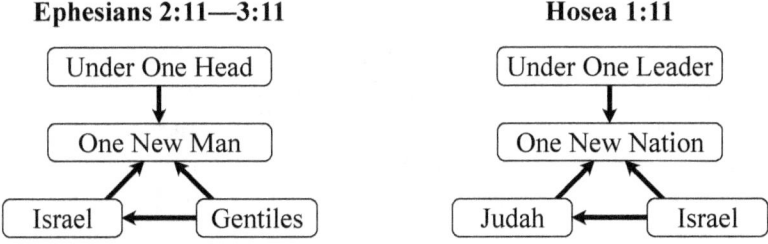

Ephesians 2:11—3:11 | **Hosea 1:11**

The hidden, mysterious church in Old Testament prophecy is announced in terms of the reunion of Israel and Judah. That is a revolutionary concept. Prophetic announcements concerning Israel in the Old Testament can, and most likely do, refer to the New Testament people of God, the church. In fact, this has long been the teaching of Bible commentators over the centuries. Pick at random any commentary from before the 1900s, or any sermon from the 1800s or earlier,[12] and you will see how widespread an understanding it was that the church was seen in Old Testament prophecies relating to Israel.

There is a beautiful consequence of this understanding. When you read verses such as Ezekiel 11:19 and Ezekiel 36:26–27, it is immediately obvious to every modern believer that they are references to the salvation that is ours in Christ.

> Then I will give them one heart, and I will put a new spirit within them, and take the stony heart out of their flesh, and give them a heart of flesh. (Ezekiel 11:19)

> I will give you a new heart and put a new spirit within you; I will take the heart of stone out of your flesh and give you a heart of flesh. I will put My Spirit within you and cause you to walk in My statutes, and you will keep My judgments and do them. (Ezekiel 36:26–27)

These are clearly Old Testament references to the covenant of grace that comes to Jew and Gentile alike in Christ. But if you read those same passages within their contexts, you will see that they talk in terms of Israel coming back into its promised land.[13] This is a difficulty for Old Testament commentators who do not see the reference to the church in the identification of Israel. The simple fact is that those passages really do refer to New Testament salvation. They are part of the mystery that is revealed in the gospel: Jew and Gentile together uniting as one body under the headship of Christ.

This single point impinges so much upon our interpretation of Bible prophecy! End time scenarios get drastically rewritten when Israel is taken as a reference to the church, the hidden mystery

---

12. If you ever get the chance, go and read some of Charles Spurgeon's inspiring commentaries on the Psalms. You will find them in his classic work, *The Treasury of David*. He sees images of the church everywhere in the Psalms.

13. Refer particularly to Ezekiel 11:17; 37:15–28.

finally revealed in the New Testament. For instance, the restoration of Israel to the promised land does not concern the formation of the modern Jewish state, but describes the salvation of God's people, Jew and Gentile alike. The surrounding of Israel in the Gog and Magog conflict does not depict war in the Middle East, but persecution of the church.

Determining the identity of prophetic Israel in this way makes a huge difference to how we read Bible prophecy. So let me answer the question, who is Israel in end times prophecy? Insofar as it relates to Old Testament prophecy, Israel is a veiled reference to the New Testament church. The fulfilment of these prophecies, though they are coined in terms of Israel, is found in the church, not in the modern Jewish nation or any other political grouping of people we might want to identify as Israel.

I need to state very clearly at this point that I am only talking about Israel in terms of Eschatology. There is a definite role that Israel plays in terms of Salvation History. Paul makes this abundantly clear in the letter to the Romans.[14] They are the literal descendants of Abraham, and though they must stand by faith like everyone else in the gospel, they have promises spoken over them that still apply. Nevertheless, though there remains a place for the nation of Israel insofar as the doctrine of Salvation is concerned, the doctrine of the Return of Christ goes elsewhere when it uses the name, Israel.

By the time you have finished this book, you will see how this first colored lens significantly underlines the testimony of Jesus. It will cause us to rally behind the gospel and believe in its power to convert nations, not just individuals.

OUR SECOND SET OF GLASSES—WHO DOES PROPHECY DIRECTLY SPEAK TO?

It is important to be aware of the historical setting of the Old Testament prophets. We tend to read their writings devotionally and in the order they are arranged in our Bibles. In doing so, we can unintentionally dismiss the impact they had on the contemporary issues

---

14. Refer Romans 3:1–2; Romans 11:1–32.

of their original audiences. Nevertheless, though the prophets addressed the current affairs of their time, some of their prophecies held promise for the distant, New Testament future. At those times, the Spirit of Christ in them bore witness that there were hidden depths to their message.

> Of this salvation the prophets have inquired and searched carefully, who prophesied of the grace that would come to you, searching what, or what manner of time, the Spirit of Christ who was in them was indicating when He testified beforehand the sufferings of Christ and the glories that would follow. (1 Peter 1:10–11)

There was something within the prophet, an inner witness, that hinted to him that his prophesying did not simply address contemporary issues. The Spirit was pointing to New Testament realities that went far beyond the circumstances of the world of the prophet. With the benefit of hindsight, we can observe many of these successive, and much later, applications of the prophets' predictions.

It is probably helpful to show you an example that highlights this repetitive, or layered, nature of prophecy. I will take a well-known example to illustrate.

> Therefore the Lord Himself will give you a sign: Behold, the virgin shall conceive and bear a Son, and shall call His name Immanuel. (Isaiah 7:14)

I am sure you recognize this prophetic announcement of Christ's virgin birth, written by Isaiah some seven centuries before Mary's conception. Yet, familiar as you may be with the passage, are you aware that within its context, the verse had an immediate fulfilment in the time of Isaiah? In some respects, it is not helpful that the NKJV capitalizes the Son. That sets the reader up to only see the reference to Christ in the prophecy. But the passage continues . . .

> Curds and honey he shall eat, that he may know to refuse the evil and choose the good. For before the child shall know to refuse the evil and choose the good, the land that you dread will be forsaken by both her kings.

Prophetic Colored Glasses

> The LORD will bring the king of Assyria upon you and your people and your father's house—days that have not come since the day that Ephraim departed from Judah. (Isaiah 7:15–17)

The prophet Isaiah spoke the whole of this prophecy to Ahaz, king of Judah, on the occasion of the siege against Judah by the nations of Assyria and Israel.[15] Part of the prophecy was to be graphically enacted in the birth of Isaiah's son to a young virgin prophetess.[16] The son was to be called Immanuel—God with us.

> Then I went to the prophetess, and she conceived and bore a son. Then the LORD said to me, "Call his name Maher-Shalal-Hash-Baz *(which means quick to plunder, swift to the spoil)*; for before the child shall have knowledge to cry 'My father' and 'My mother,' the riches of Damascus and the spoil of Samaria will be taken away before the king of Assyria." (Isaiah 8:3–4)

Though he warned King Ahaz of an Assyrian invasion, Isaiah recognized that, in some way, he was also speaking of a distant Messianic future.

> Here am I and the children whom the LORD has given me! We are for signs and wonders in Israel from the LORD of hosts, who dwells in Mount Zion. (Isaiah 8:18)

Isaiah and his children were for signs and wonders in Israel. They spoke to the immediate need of Judah in those days, and yet they foretold a day when a virgin would supernaturally give birth to One who would literally be "God with us," Immanuel.

> So all this was done that it might be fulfilled which was spoken by the Lord through the prophet, saying: *"Behold, the virgin shall be with child, and bear a Son, and they shall call His name Immanuel,"* which is translated, "God with us." (Matthew 1:22–23)

---

15. Called Ephraim in the prophecy, after the northern kingdom's principal tribe.

16. This was not a virgin birth. At the time when the prophecy was first pronounced, the girl was not yet married to Isaiah, and so was referred to as a virgin in the prophecy.

This example from Isaiah dramatically illustrates the potential for a prophecy to have more than one fulfilment. Without a doubt, this opens up the whole arena of prophetic interpretation. What was previously seen to be the one-and-only interpretation of a prophecy may simply be one of many.

The inevitable conclusion is that, though a prophecy may allude to an end time event, it does not necessarily follow that it should be expounded as speaking solely of that event. Its primary focus may be a general principle that applies to all generations alike. This can be a recipe for an expositor's nightmare, but it does have the wonderful outcome of showing God's heart in prophecy. Essentially, prophecy is more of a sermon than a prediction of events. It is a message that brings hope to people of all times and cultures, and specifically encourages them to trust in the unfailing love of God.

Our second colored lens enables us to see the power of prophecy to speak to every generation. In this way, it brings us back, time and again, to the testimony of Jesus, the spirit of prophecy.

With our colored lenses in place, then, read on and together we will explore the wonderful, challenging, and gripping world of Bible prophecy and the return of Christ.

> But he who prophesies speaks edification and exhortation and comfort to men.
>
> 1 CORINTHIANS 14:3

3

Signs of the Times

SINCE THE EARLIEST DAYS of the church, Christians have believed that Jesus would return in their very near future, despite his clear assertion that we cannot know the times or seasons related to his coming.[1] Still, every generation since Christ has seen enough evidence in its world to expect his soon return.[2] Logic alone should warn us against making such a claim.

As far as Scriptural indications go, it is just as probable that Christ will come in the year 4000 as in our lifetime. Given the fervor with which many people hold to their view of prophecy, however, that is quite possibly one of the most scandalous statements you will read in this book.

JESUS' RETURN IS AT HAND

Jesus could return at any moment. Any moment. This is the simple teaching of the New Testament.[3] As the Apostle John said at the close of the first century . . .

---

1. Acts 1:7–8.

2. Section Two, *Oracles Galore*, of Dr. Ken Chant's book, *When the Trumpet Sounds*, contains a compilation of twenty centuries of failed predictions of the nearness of Christ's return.

3. Consider Matthew 24:42–44.

The Lost Message of the End Times

> Dear children, this is the last hour; and as you have heard that the antichrist is coming, even now many antichrists have come. This is how we know that it is the last hour. (1 John 2:18)

We can say with great certainty that Jesus did not return in the days of the Apostle John or any other of the New Testament writers. Were they wrong, then, in asserting the nearness of Christ's return? If you have a high view of Scripture, the answer is clearly No, so we need to determine what it means that Jesus' return is near.

Theologically, the imminence of Christ's return means that he is ready to return, at the door, so to speak. Let me clarify the point with a diagram.

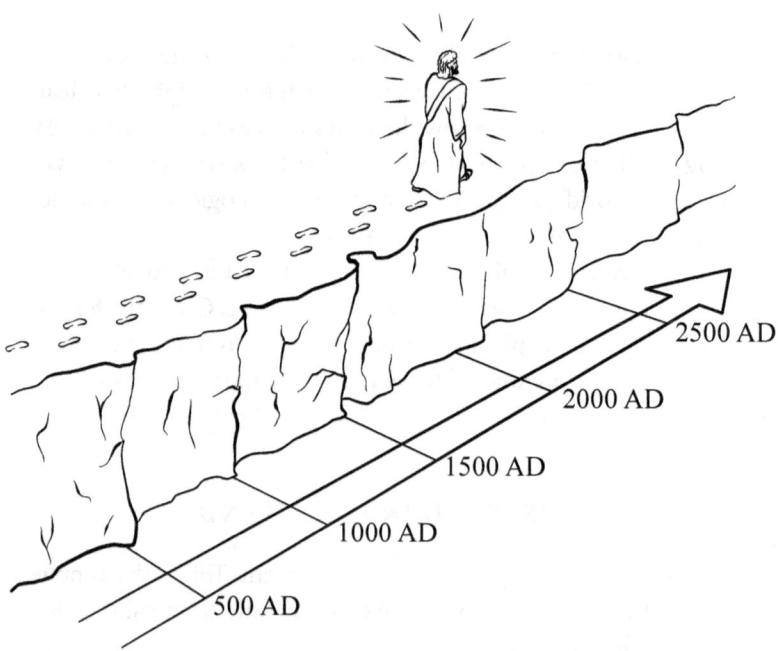

The Lord is Near

The picture is of a cliff wall. The lower plain represents our world and the upper plain is the heavenly world from which Christ will descend. The baseline of the cliff is our timeline. In the days of the apostles, Christ was walking along the top edge of the cliff, as depicted by his footsteps. When the apostles looked up, they saw Christ very near, even at the door. He was only one step, or jump down the cliff, away from us. As time progresses, he is no closer than he has always been, yet no further. And so it was true for John to say that we are living in the last hour, but that hour is necessarily of indefinite length.

The point to take to heart is that Christ could return at any moment. There is nothing holding him back except the express will and purpose of the Father. There are no prophecies which must first fall into line—Christ's return is imminent, and it has been so for some two thousand years!

WHAT OF THE SIGNS THAT INDICATE THE LORD'S VERY SOON RETURN?

The most famous text about recognizing the signs of the times is found in Matthew 24 and needs to be expounded if we are to correctly interpret the events of our world. Set on the Mount of Olives, the passage is called the Olivet Discourse by scholars and commentators. The opening verses set the scene.

> Then Jesus went out and departed from the temple, and His disciples came up to show Him the buildings of the temple. And Jesus said to them, "Do you not see all these things? Assuredly, I say to you, not one stone shall be left here upon another, that shall not be thrown down." Now as He sat on the Mount of Olives, the disciples came to Him privately, saying, "Tell us, when will these things be? And what will be the sign of Your coming, and of the end of the age?" (Matthew 24:1–3)

The disciples, marveling at the splendor of the temple, were astonished when Jesus foretold its destruction. They asked him the obvious question, "When will this happen, and what will be the sign of your coming and of the end of the age?"

To the disciples, such an extraordinary event must surely herald the time of Jesus' appearing as the Messianic King of their expectations and usher in the end of the age. They naturally thought they were asking one question. Unknown to them, however, they were asking two.

"When will the temple be destroyed?"

"What will be the sign (singular) of Christ's coming and the end of the age?"

Since Jesus knew the two events were not necessarily concurrent, his answer formed two parts. Perhaps most people are confused by Jesus' response, considering one verse refers to the first question and the next verse refers to the second, in a rambling admixture, as if Jesus answered the two questions and then shuffled it all up to form a jumbled mess. They end up building a commentary that makes Jesus sound, at best, vague, if not personally baffled.

Our problem is that we fail to recognize the literary background of first century Judea. Jesus' response needs to be understood against this background. What you are probably unaware of is that there is a great similarity between the language of the Olivet Discourse and the popular apocalyptic literature of Jesus' time.[4] More importantly, when we study his answer in this light, we find that Jesus made a logical and straightforward response to his disciples' questions.

In verses 4–8, Jesus explained that the destruction of the temple would not necessarily indicate his immediate return. Verses 9–34 addresses the disciples' first question, that concerning the destruction of the temple. The rest of the discourse, from verse 35 onwards, deals with his return.

Let us look closely at how it all pieces together. I will take some time on this, guiding you through verse by verse, because this is such a pivotal passage in our understanding of the end times.

---

4. Daniel and Revelation are Biblical examples of apocalyptic writing, but there were many non-Biblical books which incorporated similar language and imagery in depicting cataclysmic events.

THE DESTRUCTION OF THE TEMPLE AND CHRIST'S RETURN ARE NOT CONCURRENT

> And Jesus answered and said to them: "Take heed that no one deceives you. For many will come in My name, saying, 'I am the Christ,' and will deceive many. And you will hear of wars and rumors of wars. See that you are not troubled; for all these things must come to pass, but the end is not yet. For nation will rise against nation, and kingdom against kingdom. And there will be famines, pestilences, and earthquakes in various places. All these are the beginning of sorrows." (Matthew 24:4–8)

In these opening remarks, Jesus warned against misinterpreting the signs of the times. Social and natural disasters, so often read as portents of the end of the age, are the beginning of birth pains, not the end. They certainly are signs that the end must come, and indeed that it is coming, but they are not signs of its immediacy at all!

The tragedy is that most people, Christian and non-Christian alike, fail to see such calamities as signs. When we hear of a disaster here, or a conflict there, we are supposed to take them as evidence that the world must, of necessity, have a radical rebuild! Though they are not signs that the end is about to occur, they are signs that the end must occur. The sobering truth we miss is that with Christ's return comes judgment as well as salvation.

Take note, then, of these signs—hear Christ's voice in them. If you are not a believer, give your life to him now. If you are a believer, make the most of every opportunity to be a living example of what it means to be a believer.

JESUS' ANSWER TO THE FIRST QUESTION— WHEN WILL THE TEMPLE BE DESTROYED?

> Then they will deliver you up to tribulation and kill you, and you will be hated by all nations for My name's sake. And then many will be offended, will betray one another, and will hate one another. Then many false prophets will

> rise up and deceive many. And because lawlessness will abound, the love of many will grow cold. But he who endures to the end shall be saved. (Matthew 24:9-13)

These verses speak of the persecution that the apostles and the first century church would experience in the years prior to the Roman-Jewish war that saw the temple's destruction.[5] (The NKJV uses the word tribulation in this passage. It is a term that features heavily in today's popular dispensationalist view of the return of Christ. I devote a whole section to it in chapter 5, *The War of Armageddon*.)

> And this gospel of the kingdom will be preached in all the world as a witness to all the nations, and then the end will come. (Matthew 24:14)

Many people look for a fulfilment of this prophecy in our own day. It is challenging, however, to learn that Paul considered this already to have been fulfilled by the middle of the first century!

> If indeed you continue in the faith, grounded and steadfast, and are not moved away from the hope of the gospel which you heard, which was preached to every creature under heaven, of which I, Paul, became a minister. (Colossians 1:23)

The gospel has been preached to every creature under heaven! Paul made this claim somewhere around 60AD, and yet it is obvious that the entire globe had not been absolutely and thoroughly missionized—indeed, it never has been. Was Paul wrong? Or being immersed in the language and idioms of New Testament times, would he have had a better understanding of what Jesus meant when he said the whole world would have the gospel preached to it before the end?[6]

---

5. Christians were severely persecuted in those early days. For New Testament examples, consider Acts 4; 5:17-42; 7:55—8:3.

6. The Jewish use of language is not as pedantic as English can be. For example, in Acts 2:5 it is not needed to be understood that each and every nation was represented—indeed they could not have been. But the Scriptural statement is still accurate. We know what it means.

In other words, in this verse, so widely regarded as a key element of the end times, Jesus was still answering the disciples' first question. Before the temple would be destroyed, the church would missionize the world amid periods of persecution. And he was right.

> Therefore when you see the 'abomination of desolation,' spoken of by Daniel the prophet, standing in the holy place (whoever reads, let him understand). (Matthew 24:15)

Jesus referred to Daniel's prophecy in which he talked about the *abomination that causes desolation*. You will find it in Daniel 11:31 and Daniel 12:11. What confuses many commentators is that neither of those passages spoke of the end times, but instead found fulfilment in the desecration of the temple by Antiochus Epiphanes in 167BC. Describing that event, the writer of the apocryphal history book of 1 Maccabees wrote:

> On every side of the sanctuary they shed innocent blood; they even defiled the sanctuary... And the king sent letters by messengers to Jerusalem and the cities of Judah; he directed them to follow customs strange to the land, to forbid burnt offerings and sacrifices and drink offerings in the sanctuary, to profane Sabbaths and feasts, to defile the sanctuary and the priests, to build altars and sacred precincts and shrines for idols, to sacrifice swine and unclean animals, and to leave their sons uncircumcised. They were to make themselves abominable by everything unclean and profane, so that they would forget the law and change all the ordinances... Now on the fifteenth day of Chislev, in the one hundred and forty-fifth year *(167BC)*, they erected a desolating sacrilege upon the altar of burnt offering. They also built altars in the surrounding cities of Judah, and burned incense at the doors of the houses and in the streets. The books of the law which they found they tore to pieces and burned with fire. (1 Maccabees 1:37, 44-49, 54-56)[7]

---

7. Revised Standard Version of the Bible, Apocrypha, copyright 1957; The Third and Fourth Books of the Maccabees and Psalm 151, copyright 1977 by the Division of Christian Education of the National Council of the churches of Christ in the United States of America. Used by permission. All rights reserved.

Jesus saw in this a similarity to what would occur again in the days of the Roman destruction of the temple.[8] A paraphrase of Jesus' words will help you understand what Jesus was saying in this claim.

What was done to Jerusalem by Antiochus, as foretold by Daniel, will happen again. So when you see a repetition of those events which came in fulfilment of Daniel's prophecy at the time of Antiochus, then know that it is time to flee.

This was fulfilled when the Roman Commander, Titus, entered the temple in April 70AD, seizing its treasures and razing it to the ground.

> ... then let those who are in Judea flee to the mountains. Let him who is on the housetop not go down to take anything out of his house. And let him who is in the field not go back to get his clothes. But woe to those who are pregnant and to those who are nursing babies in those days! And pray that your flight may not be in winter or on the Sabbath. For then there will be great tribulation, such as has not been since the beginning of the world until this time, no, nor ever shall be. And unless those days were shortened, no flesh would be saved; but for the elect's sake those days will be shortened. (Matthew 24:16–22)

This is a greatly misunderstood passage, but Jesus was describing the fall of Jerusalem. How then could he call it *great tribulation such as has not been since the beginning of the world until this time*?

We use language in a very different way to people of other times and other cultures. Detailing the Roman assault on Jerusalem, the second century Jewish historian, Josephus, wrote ...

> I shall therefore speak my mind here at once briefly that neither did any other city ever suffer such miseries, nor did any age ever breed a generation more fruitful in wickedness than this was from the beginning of the world.[9]

---

8. This is an example of the repetitive nature of prophecy, that though it may speak specifically to one particular event, it may be applied to other times where circumstances are similar.

9. *Wars*, 5, 10. The quote is from Chant, *The Return*, 89.

Signs of the Times

This is very close to Jesus' language. From our point of view, we could certainly argue the historical accuracy of such a statement and furnish many examples of wars that were as horrific, if not far worse, than that in first century Judea. But that would miss the cultural use of language. Josephus gives us an insight into how to understand Jesus' description of the distress of those days. It really was a time of unequalled distress!

Failing to recognize this cultural and linguistic context, modern expositors conclude that the passage has not been fulfilled and they are forced to look for a future fulfilment. The simple truth, however, is that it has come and gone a long, long time ago.

> Then if anyone says to you, "Look, here is the Christ!" or "There!" do not believe it. For false christs and false prophets will rise and show great signs and wonders to deceive, if possible, even the elect. See, I have told you beforehand. Therefore if they say to you, "Look, He is in the desert!" do not go out; or "Look, He is in the inner rooms!" do not believe it. (Matthew 24:23-26)

It is likely always true that in times of national turmoil, false prophets step into the public arena and gain notoriety. Jerusalem's fall supplied just such an occasion.[10] Jesus warned his disciples, and with them all first century Judean believers, not to be taken in by spurious claims from false christs and false prophets. There would be no mistaking his return.

> For as the lightning comes from the east and flashes to the west, so also will the coming of the Son of Man be. For wherever the carcass is, there the eagles will be gathered together. (Matthew 24:27-28)

To this point, we see that Jesus logically and methodically answered the disciples' question regarding the destruction of the temple. His message was clear: the destruction of Jerusalem will provide no indication of his return. The next verses, however, may not be as clear to many. Let us see what Jesus meant by them.

---

10. It is sobering to consider that such false prophets and christs were even around in the turbulent days in which Jesus ministered. See Acts 5:36-37; Acts 8:9-13; Acts 21:38.

> Immediately after the tribulation of those days the sun will be darkened, and the moon will not give its light; the stars will fall from heaven, and the powers of the heavens will be shaken. Then the sign of the Son of Man will appear in heaven, and then all the tribes of the earth will mourn, and they will see the Son of Man coming on the clouds of heaven with power and great glory. (Matthew 24:29–30)

Being apocalyptic in nature, these verses are often interpreted as referring to the Second Coming and feature regularly in expositions on Eschatology. For that reason, we need to study them closely because they have nothing to do with the return of Christ. A glaring mistake is made when expositors pay little or no attention to two verses from Isaiah, one which Jesus directly quoted and a second that he alluded to. Let us look at his claim again.

> Immediately after the tribulation of those days the sun will be darkened, and the moon will not give its light; the stars will fall from heaven, and the powers of the heavens will be shaken. (Matthew 24:29)

Now come with me to the book of Isaiah.

> For the stars of heaven and their constellations will not give their light; the sun will be darkened in its going forth, and the moon will not cause its light to shine. (Isaiah 13:10)

Jesus quoted from this verse, yet it finds its place within a prophecy that related to the fall of the ancient Babylonian Empire. Whatever we are to make of the sun, moon, and stars not giving off their light, one thing is certain: If it could be said of the fall of Babylon in 539BC, it was not meant to be taken literally.

> All the host of heaven shall be dissolved, and the heavens shall be rolled up like a scroll; all their host shall fall down as the leaf falls from the vine, and as fruit falling from a fig tree. (Isaiah 34:4)

Jesus clearly alluded to this verse when talking of the stars falling from heaven and the powers of the heavens being shaken. In its context, however, it is part of a prophecy that particularly applied to the ancient people of Edom.[11]

That is significant! Both of Isaiah's prophecies had long since been fulfilled when Jesus used them. How are we to understand Jesus' claim, then?

The language employs distinctly Jewish apocalyptic imagery for the overthrow and fall of political powers. While such language can certainly foreshadow the end of this age, Jesus' obvious intention was to describe the 70AD fall of Jerusalem.

> Then the sign of the Son of Man will appear in heaven, and then all the tribes of the earth will mourn, and they will see the Son of Man coming on the clouds of heaven with power and great glory. (Matthew 24:30)

By now, you already know that I am going to show you how this relates to the destruction of the temple. And you are probably wondering how on earth that could be so. So let me break it down for you step by step.

First, let me show you how to understand *all the tribes of the earth*. The expression literally translates as *all the tribes of the land*. This is an appropriate description of the first century inhabitants of Judea and indeed, at the fall of Jerusalem, it was an intensely mournful time for God-fearing Jews.

And then comes Jesus' famous prediction. The people of Judea will see the Son of Man coming on the clouds of heaven. Surely this indicates the visible return of Christ!? Or does it? To answer this question, we must take a step backwards and determine the disciples' understanding of what it meant for Jesus to *come*.

You see, at the time of the Olivet Discourse, the disciples were not even aware that Christ would die, let alone rise from the dead, let alone ascend into heaven and one day return from there. What, then, did they mean when they asked Christ for the sign of his coming in their original question? They did not even know he was going! Clearly, the expression did not mean for them what it means for us.

Without a doubt, they understood their question as referring to Jesus coming into political power. We can certainly agree that

---

11. Refer Isaiah 34:5–6.

Jesus did not use the word in that way; his Kingdom is not earthly, and its impact goes beyond secular politics. But there was another contemporary Jewish usage of the expression, one which is different to what the disciples meant and, significantly, also different to what Christians understand by it.

Jesus' description of the Son of Man coming on the clouds uses the same language and imagery as Daniel 7.

> I was watching in the night visions, and behold, One like the Son of Man, coming with the clouds of heaven! He came to the Ancient of Days, and they brought Him near before Him. Then to Him was given dominion and glory and a kingdom, that all peoples, nations, and languages should serve Him. His dominion is an everlasting dominion, which shall not pass away, and His kingdom the one which shall not be destroyed. (Daniel 7:13–14)

The similarity between Daniel's vision and Jesus' expression is obvious. And because of this, many make the mistake of thinking they are talking of the same thing. But that could not be further from the truth.

Both passages depict the Son of Man coming on the clouds of heaven, but in Daniel's vision, the Son of Man is led before the Ancient of Days, not bursting through the heavens to the earth. It is a heavenly setting. The two are not the same.

In Daniel's vision, the One like the Son of Man was ushered before the Ancient of Days. And it was there that he was given dominion, glory, and a kingdom. Let me ask a question: When was Jesus given dominion, glory, and a kingdom? The answer lies in the short space of time between the crucifixion and resurrection of Christ, after which Jesus could say, "All authority has been given to Me in heaven and on earth." (Matthew 28:18)[12]

---

12. It is an interesting affirmation of Christ's. "All authority has been given to Me, therefore go." Why did he say that at that time, just before his ascension? Surely, he had that authority beforehand in the time of his earthly ministry? But we miss an important truth. In the crucifixion and the resurrection, Jesus truly had become the "firstborn among many brothers." Before then, he was the Saviour, on mission to secure our redemption. But after his victory on the cross, it was time for him to delegate his global mission to his people. Daniel's

It was at the cross that Jesus secured victory over the devil,[13] and it was because of the redemption that was then brought to light, that he could present his victory to the Father, and in so doing receive from him all authority in heaven and on earth. Daniel's vision certainly spoke about Jesus, but it concerned his work on the cross, not his return.

As used by Daniel, then, the expression *coming with the clouds of heaven* was not a physical riding of Christ in the clouds.[14] It foretold God's powerful act of confirming the Son's Lordship over his Kingdom as the first of God's New Creation people.[15]

When Jesus said, then, that the Jews will see the Son of Man coming on the clouds of heaven with power and great glory, he was using the expression in the same theological sense as Daniel. In conferring the Kingdom to Jesus at the cross, the Father asserted the Son's authority over all those who sought his crucifixion. In the destruction of Jerusalem, the Father once again asserted the Son's authority over those same people, who had so foolishly said, "Let his blood be on us!"[16]

The gospel was first proclaimed to the Jews, both in Christ's earthly ministry and in the witness of the early church. Yet by their continual rejection, the Jews incurred God's judgment. This was historically fulfilled in the destruction of Jerusalem and is depicted in terms of the Son coming in the clouds.

---

vision is significant in this regard. It shows some of what happened after Jesus' death. On that day, having thrown open heaven's gates, and with the thief on the cross the first in line to be with Christ in Paradise, he was ushered into the presence of the Father, there to have conferred upon him all authority in heaven and earth. Or as Daniel put it, to receive dominion, glory, and a kingdom.

13. Colossians 2:15.

14. As a side note, and not of any real import to our discussion on Eschatology, we could rightly interpret the *clouds of heaven* as the company of those redeeemed by the efficacy of the cross. Hebrews 12:2, in summing up the overview of the multitude of Old Testament saints, calls them a *cloud of witnesses*.

15. Daniel 7:13–14 compares exactly with Matthew 28:18.

16. And all the people answered and said, "His blood be on us and on our children." (Matthew 27:25)

> And He will send His angels with a great sound of a trumpet, and they will gather together His elect from the four winds, from one end of heaven to the other. (Matthew 24:31)

Historically, we know that with the commencement of Jewish-Roman hostilities, the Christians of Jerusalem fled Judea. Their dispersion actually aided the furthering of the gospel. The trumpet call is the proclamation of the gospel[17] and the angels spoken of are those first Christians who spread it.[18]

> Now learn this parable from the fig tree: When its branch has already become tender and puts forth leaves, you know that summer is near. So you also, when you see all these things, know that it is near—at the doors! Assuredly, I say to you, this generation will by no means pass away till all these things take place. (Matthew 24:32–34)

This is the conclusion of Jesus' response to the disciples' first question. *This generation* would see the outworking of God's judgment on the nation of Israel and the destruction of Jerusalem's temple. And it would be as obvious as the approach of summer. But who did Jesus mean by *this generation*?

It is an easy question to answer, since Jesus used the expression often. In each case, he applied it to the generation of his audience.[19] So we can confidently say that the generation he spoke of in the passage we are studying was the generation he was speaking to. Contrary to a lot of popular teaching in today's world, he was not talking about an end time generation, nor was he talking of the Jewish race collectively. He simply stated that the generation of those first disciples would not pass away before the events surrounding the destruction of the temple were fulfilled. And he was correct.

---

17. As used in Isaiah 27:13, it refers to the calling of Israel's exiles.

18. The word translated as *angel* simply means *messenger* and does not always refer to what we would call angels. In some instances, people are referred to as angels. See for example Revelation 1:20.

19. Consider Matthew 11:16; Matthew 12:41–42; Matthew 12:45; Mark 8:12; Mark 8:38; Luke 11:50–51; Luke 17:25.

Within forty years of Jesus' discourse—the timespan of a generation—the temple at Jerusalem was gone.

JESUS' ANSWER TO THE SECOND QUESTION— WHAT WILL BE THE SIGN OF HIS RETURN?

Our discussion so far has made one thing clear: many of our modern beliefs of the Second Coming are based on misguided interpretations of Jesus' words. What can we say, then, of the return of Christ? The answer to the second part of the disciples' question, that referring to his coming again, is given from verse 35 through to the end of chapter 25.

Now here is a remarkable observation. All Bible commentators recognize the obvious rhetorical shift in Jesus' discourse that commences at verse 35.[20] They recognize that from that point on, Jesus' words are less complicated, less predictive, less apocalyptic in nature. Remember: there were two distinct questions. And now we find that Jesus' response is in two distinct parts. For my mind, this is the clearest evidence that Jesus answered the two questions logically and in sequence. No confusion was intended in his reply.

> Heaven and earth will pass away, but My words will by no means pass away. But of that day and hour no one knows, not even the angels of heaven, but My Father only. (Matthew 24:35–36)

Jesus only gave one answer to the second half of the disciples' question. In chapter 6, *When Christ Rules the World*, I explain what the Bible really teaches about the millennium. I do not want to jump the gun on that but allow me to make one small observation up front. The disciples believed they were asking one question. Jesus knew better and supplied two answers. Yet it could rightly be

---

20. For instance, the NIV has Matthew 24:1–35 under the heading *Signs of the End of the Age* and verse 36 onwards under the heading *The Day and Hour Unknown*. The headings are not helpful, and betray the translators' theologies, but one thing is obvious; the translators recognized that the discourse is in two sections.

argued from the viewpoint of a premillennialist interpretation of Eschatology, that there were actually three questions.

- When will this be?
- What will be the sign of your coming?
- What will be the sign of the end of the age?

For Jesus, however, there really were only two questions, so two answers. One concerned the destruction of Jerusalem and the second concerned the end of the age, with his return and the commencement of the new heavens and new earth. In Jesus' understanding, then, when he appears, it will mark the beginning of eternity. This does not accord with a premillennialist framework.

In discussing the sign of his return, then, Christ affirms that it really will happen. "Heaven and earth will pass away." But there will be no sign. The return of Christ will occur when it is least expected, a time known only by the Father.

There is more to be said on this matter, but before I take you any further, I want to make a small diversion that I think will be helpful for you.

CRISIS IN THE EARLY CHURCH

To this point, we have only looked at the Olivet Discourse as it is recorded in Matthew's Gospel. The historical background to the Gospels as a whole is important, however, and is instructive for how we should read the Olivet Discourse.

The first Gospel to be written was Mark's. There is so much we could say about the genre, message, and importance of these early written accounts of the life and teachings of Christ. It will be helpful for you to know that the Gospels are much more than simple eye-witness accounts. They are portraits of Christ, paintings done with words. In writing his Gospel, Mark took the teachings and ministry of Christ and arranged them in such a way that he could emphasize an aspect of Christ that he wanted his readers to see.

Luke and Matthew both picked up on what Mark had done and reworded the account[21] in such a way as to paint their own portraits of Christ.[22] Understanding the Gospels as paintings, rather than photographs, is critical. You do not take three paintings of an individual and overlay them to get the true and complete picture. When we marry the Gospels together, trying to make everything harmonize, we construct a fifth Gospel, and in fact, lose all four. But that is for another book.

What is important for us, at this point, is to understand what happened in the Judean church when Jerusalem fell in 70AD. At that time, Mark was the only Gospel that had been written. They had not read the passage we are studying from Matthew 24—it had not been written yet. When the early Judean Christians read the Olivet Discourse, as it appears in Mark's Gospel, here is the question they heard from the mouth of the disciples:

> Tell us, when will these things be? And what will be the sign when all these things will be fulfilled? (Mark 13:4)

You can understand at once the confusion that fell upon the early church. Some, at least, of Jesus' reply had to do with his return. You do not have to be a scholar to see that. But the disciples' question, as Mark recorded it, was a simple one. It spoke only of the destruction of the temple. So the early church assumed that whenever Jerusalem should fall, Jesus would come back. And Jerusalem fell. And the temple was desecrated. Just like Jesus said. But Jesus did not come back!

They were left with the awkward question: Did Jesus get it wrong?

Partly to address this, but mostly to paint their own portraits of Christ, both Matthew and Luke focused in on that Olivet Discourse.

We have already discussed Matthew's rendition of the disciples' question. It is different to how Mark recorded it.

---

21. Putting the emphasis of the story on different aspects of Christ's Person and work.

22. These three are known amongst theologians as the Synoptic Gospels. They "look with the same eye."

> Tell us, when will these things be? And what will be the sign of Your coming, and of the end of the age?" (Matthew 24:3)

It is not that Mark was inaccurate in his telling of the account. Living at a time well before the Roman assault on Jerusalem, it was not on his horizon to be pedantic with the specific language that the disciples had used. They themselves, at the time of the discussion with Jesus, felt they were only asking the one question. Mark faithfully reproduced that: "When will these things be? And what will be the sign when all these things will be fulfilled?"

But after the faith crisis that shook the first century church, Matthew saw the need to clarify the disciples' question, the way they had literally asked it, not the way they had meant it. It is as if Matthew was saying to the first century church, "The disciples didn't realize it, but they actually asked two unrelated questions: When will the temple be destroyed? What will be the sign of Jesus' coming?"

Luke dealt with the confusion in an entirely different manner. He split the Olivet Discourse into two and placed each part in a different section of his Gospel. In this way, he completely separated Jesus' comments about the temple from those concerning his return. By approaching the matter this way, Luke could keep Mark's original question without altering the way it was phrased.

> So they asked Him, saying, "Teacher, but when will these things be? And what sign will there be when these things are about to take place?" (Luke 21:7)

Do not be confused by the paragraph headings in your modern Bible. None of these are in the original text. For example, many prints of the NKJV have the headings *The Signs of the Times and the End of the Age* (Luke 21:7-19); *The Destruction of Jerusalem* (Luke 21:20-24); *The Coming of the Son of Man* (Luke 21:25-28); and *The Parable of the Fig Tree* (Luke 21:29-33). These reflect the theological bias of the translators, not the Biblical authors. Simply put, they got it wrong because they neither understood Jesus' answer nor why Luke split the Olivet Discourse into two.

We have already seen from our discussion of the same passage as it appears in Matthew's Gospel, that none of the discussion of Luke 21 refers to the Second Coming at all. Like Matthew, Luke 21 follows Mark's account closely. The natural break in Jesus' discourse, as we have noted earlier, is marked by the statement that finds its place in verse 33 of Luke 21.

> Heaven and earth will pass away, but My words will by no means pass away. (Luke 21:33)

The rest of the Olivet Discourse, that both Mark and Matthew keep in the one context, Luke records in a discussion with the Pharisees about the coming of the Kingdom of God. You can read it in Luke 17:20–37. In doing this, Luke focused the early church back on to what Jesus was really saying. It was as if he said, "Jesus did not say he would come back when the temple was destroyed. You do not need to have a crisis of faith just because the Romans have fulfilled one of Jesus' predictions but not another."

Finally, we have John's Gospel. John wrote decades after Matthew and Luke. He did not even record the Olivet Discourse. Interestingly, however, he took the language of Eschatology and applied it to the here and now.[23] By doing this, he addressed another issue that faced the church at the turn of the first century: they were so focused on the Second Coming that they forgot their purpose, what it was they were called to do—preach the gospel. Given our current-day fascination with the signs of the times, I think we would

---

23. The principal features of Eschatology are used as current realities in John's Gospel. Judgment Day—the people already have been judged (John 3:18); they do not believe. The Resurrection of the Dead—those who are dead have come out of their graves already (John 5:24–29); they have heard his voice and believed. New dwellings in the eternal Kingdom—many mansions prepared for us by Christ (John 14:1–3); the context relates to the gift of the Spirit and is akin to Paul's revelation that we are seated in heavenly places right now. The Return of Christ—he will not leave us as orphans but come to us (John 14:15–18); in the context, he is talking about the gift of the Spirit. Eternal Life—redefined in terms of our intimate union with the Father and the Son (John 17:3). Be clear, however: John is not saying these central tenets of Eschatology are wrong, he simply wants to get our focus off the return of Christ and onto outworking the current realities of the Kingdom of God.

all do well to listen to John on that matter. There is work to do and a gospel to preach and a life empowered by the Spirit to live.

I trust that was a helpful diversion and gives a little more clarity into our discussion on the Olivet Discourse. Let us return now to our exploration of Matthew's account of this important part of Christ's teaching.

ARE WE PREPARED FOR HIS COMING?

The purpose of Eschatology is not to predict the events surrounding the time when Jesus returns. Its message intends to cause people to consider whether they have good reason to be assured of God's favor. As in the parables of chapter 25, which are meant to be read as part of the Olivet Discourse, the question to be asked is, "Are we ready?" Are we like the foolish virgins who have no relationship with Christ or are we like the wise?[24] Are we like the lazy servants who do not value the gift of salvation and so bury it, not allowing it to produce fruit in their lives, or are we like the diligent servants?[25] Are we ready to stand before the Judge?[26]

THE NATURE OF CHRIST'S RETURN

Firstly, no one will know the day or hour.

> Heaven and earth will pass away, but My words will by no means pass away. But of that day and hour no one knows, not even the angels of heaven, but My Father only. (Matthew 24:35–36)

No one knows about that day. What day? The day heaven and earth pass away![27]

---

24. Matthew 25:1–13.
25. Matthew 25:14–30.
26. Matthew 25:31–46.
27. Personally, I find the force of the statement is made more clear if the literal *about* is used in place of our English *of* used in most translations. The verse reads, *Heaven and earth will pass away, but My words will by no means*

> Watch therefore, for you do not know what hour your Lord is coming. (Matthew 24:42)

Secondly, he will return as Judge.

> But as the days of Noah were, so also will the coming of the Son of Man be. For as in the days before the flood, they were eating and drinking, marrying and giving in marriage, until the day that Noah entered the ark, and did not know until the flood came and took them all away, so also will the coming of the Son of Man be. Then two men will be in the field: one will be taken and the other left. Two women will be grinding at the mill: one will be taken and the other left. (Matthew 24:37–41)

This passage is popularly used in support of the theory that the church vanishes at Christ's return.[28] This is not at all what the Scripture is saying. The reference to the days of Noah is to emphasize the unpreparedness of the world when Christ returns. It is not intended to give a methodology of how Christ returns. That aside, however, Christ's words say quite the opposite of a secret rapture. In referring to the days of Noah, Jesus reflects on the judgment that fell upon the wicked. The flood took them away. Did you notice Jesus' turn of phrase? It shows his emphasis on God's judgment. It was the wicked who were taken in the days of Noah. The ones who were left at the end of that judgment were the righteous; everyone else was dead.

Now look at how Jesus compared that to his return. As in the days of Noah, those who reject the offer of salvation will be taken. He is referring to judgment, not rapture. Two men will be in the field. One will be taken in God's judgment, the other left.

Do you feel the weight of that?

When he returns, it will be just as it was in the days of Noah. There will be those who are saved and those who are taken![29]

---

pass away. But about that day and hour no one knows, not even the angels in heaven, but My Father only.

28. The theory is popular amongst the Dispensationalist school of interpretation and is known as the Secret Rapture.

29. Compare with 2 Thessalonians 1:7–10.

You might ask, however, that even if Jesus did not talk about the rapture in the Olivet Discourse, surely Paul did in 1 Thessalonians?

> For the Lord Himself will descend from heaven with a shout, with the voice of an archangel, and with the trumpet of God. And the dead in Christ will rise first. Then we who are alive and remain shall be caught up together with them in the clouds to meet the Lord in the air. And thus we shall always be with the Lord. (1 Thessalonians 4:16–17)

In chapter 5, *The War of Armageddon*, I will explain in detail how the New Testament Greek language uses the definite article, *the*. But enough for me to say right now that in 1 Thessalonians 4:16–17 quoted above, there is no word *the* before *clouds*. That does not mean that *caught up together with them in the clouds* is a wrong translation, but it could just as rightly be translated *caught up together with them in clouds*. Without the definite article, the sense is completely different. The way it reads in your modern translation, you would think that we are caught away into the sky to meet the Lord in the clouds as he returns. It certainly would be interesting if that is, indeed, what it is saying. At the resurrection, there will be billions of Christians raised from the dead. It would have to be a cloud of global proportions for us all to be with him in the clouds. But of course, just considering what such a reception party would look like—billions of Christians rising to meet Christ as he returns—there certainly would be clouds of us![30]

What Paul is saying in 1 Thessalonians is that we shall certainly rise, be *caught up* as he says, to meet the Lord. But this will not be a secret rapture of the church. As visible as Christ's ascension was, so will be his return.[31] And we will be his reception party.

---

30. Therefore we also, since we are surrounded by so great a cloud of witnesses, let us lay aside every weight, and the sin which so easily ensnares us, and let us run with endurance the race that is set before us. (Hebrews 12:1).

31. Now when He had spoken these things, while they watched, He was taken up, and a cloud received Him out of their sight. And while they looked steadfastly toward heaven as He went up, behold, two men stood by them in white apparel, who also said, "Men of Galilee, why do you stand gazing up into heaven? This same Jesus, who was taken up from you into heaven, will so come

> When the Son of Man comes in His glory, and all the holy angels with Him, then He will sit on the throne of His glory. All the nations will be gathered before Him, and He will separate them one from another, as a shepherd divides his sheep from the goats. And He will set the sheep on His right hand, but the goats on the left . . . And these will go away into everlasting punishment, but the righteous into eternal life. (Matthew 25:31–33, 46)

We all stand before Christ. All of us! The nations are gathered, and Christ separates the people. This is going to happen. Be ready! He will separate us based on our actions, how we care for others. He takes our works of love for others as being towards him. Salvation is the unmerited gift of grace, not works, but our actions betray whether we have truly received that gift. It changes us irrevocably.

The wicked will go to eternal punishment and the righteous to eternal life. Take note, this is one event—one judgment of both the righteous and the unrighteous.[32] In the resurrection, then, the righteous will rise to eternal life and the wicked to eternal punishment.[33]

SO THEN, WHAT PROPHECIES ARE YET TO BE FULFILLED?

There is only one prophecy awaiting fulfilment and that is Christ's actual return. He is ready right now. Nothing holds him back except God's mercy. Jesus could come in one minute or one thousand years and no one can know otherwise.

This is not a question for us to speculate over—it is for us to be humble and obedient, and to be found doing what we are called to do. We should live our lives in the knowledge that he could come at

---

in like manner as you saw Him go into heaven." (Acts 1:9–11).

32. This is contrary to popular beliefs and teachings surrounding the nature of the resurrection of the dead and how it relates to the millennium. We will look at this in more detail in chapter 6, *When Christ Rules the World*. But for now, I just want you to see that Jesus' Olivet Discourse says nothing of two judgments separated in time, one of Christians and one of the unrighteous.

33. See also Daniel 12:2; Acts 24:15; Revelation 20:11–15.

any moment, but plan and believe for future generations recognizing that he may not come back for another two thousand years.

So let me ask you bluntly: If he came back in two minutes' time, would he find you faithfully outworking his individual call on your life or would you be ashamed? If you need to change your attitude or lifestyle, do it right now while you have the opportunity because there is a day that God has appointed, known only to him, in which he will judge the whole world. You and I really will stand before him! That can either be the thrill or dread of eternity; it is up to you. Choose wisely.

On the flipside to that, if you could know that his return was still another two thousand years away, would that change how you are sowing into future generations, laying the foundations of a better tomorrow today? Do not waste the time you have. Listen to his voice. Do what he says. And think beyond your limited timespan.

> Beloved, now we are children of God; and it has not yet been revealed what we shall be, but we know that when He is revealed, we shall be like Him, for we shall see Him as He is. And everyone who has this hope in Him purifies himself, just as He is pure.
>
> 1 JOHN 3:2–3

4

Uncovering the Apocalypse

BEING THE ONLY BOOK of the New Testament that is solely given to prophecy, John's Revelation is of considerable importance to our understanding of Eschatology. It is full of intrigue, yet it is perhaps the most confusing book of the Bible. It seems to do anything but live up to its name, the Revelation.[1] This is because we do not understand the body of literature it is a part of, given that it is a genre of writing that is not existent in our modern world.

In this chapter, I will guide you through the literary form of the Revelation, but before we look in depth at how to make sense of this exciting and powerful portion of Scripture, let us establish some guiding principles.

- It was written during a time of intense persecution of Christians. John wrote the book while imprisoned on the Isle of Patmos in the Aegean Sea just off the coast of Asia Minor—modern day Turkey. The seven churches that feature in chapters 2 and 3 were located nearby in a significant hotspot of that persecution. As you read through the Revelation, remember that its first readers were suffering Christians, facing death and imprisonment because of their faith in Christ. You may

---

1. The name is taken from the first word in the original Greek manuscript of the book, *apokalupsis*, from which we get our English word *apocalypse*. It simply means *the uncovering* or *the disclosing*, hence the Revelation.

not understand how various images are to be interpreted, but as you read the book, constantly ask yourself: How would this make a suffering, persecuted Christian feel? It will be an enlightening question for you to reflect on. You will find that the Revelation inspires hope and consolation in the face of persecution and announces the victory of the church despite the suffering it may experience as it outworks its global mission.

- The Revelation contains literally hundreds of allusions to the Old Testament. If you are not thoroughly acquainted with the Old Testament, you will miss many of these. Keep in mind, John was a first century Jew. As a boy, he had done years of study in the Torah, the Prophets, and the Writings. He was thoroughly versed in our Old Testament. If you want a detailed understanding of the Revelation, you will need to become as familiar with the Old Testament as John was. But do not despair, even for the uninitiated, the essential message—the complete and ultimate victory of the Lamb—sounds loud and clear.

- The key to understanding the Revelation is in recognizing it to be a book of images. These images are not meant to be taken literally. John does not intend you to look for a fantasy world of beasts, trumpets, bowls, wars, and foreboding riders on horses. These were never meant to be anything other than symbols.

- Another helpful guideline to adopt will be to let clear Bible teaching interpret the symbolism of the Revelation.[2] If a vision in the Revelation seems to contradict a plain New Testament teaching, we need to interpret the Revelation passage, not reinterpret what was obvious elsewhere.[3]

2. The Westminster Confession has an excellent article of faith on this matter. "The infallible standard for the interpretation of the Bible is the Bible itself. And so any question about the true and complete sense of a passage in the Bible (which is a unified whole) can be answered by referring to other passages which speak more plainly." The Westminster Shorter Catechism, Chapter 1, Article 9. By permission of Reformed Theological Seminary and Presbyterian and Reformed Publishing Company.

3. This is particularly important when seeking to understand the two

- It is also helpful to understand that the visions of the Revelation do not form a continuous chronological sequence. Prophetic books make up a large part of our Bible. For the most part, these are in our Old Testament and, like the Revelation, they also are full of visions. Of course, many of those visions referred entirely to events of the ancient world and, therefore, found fulfilment in the days before Christ. But they were not fulfilled in the same sequence in which they were written! The visions were not placed in chronological order. That is the way of the writings of the prophets. And John is no different. The Revelation is not one solitary vision whose fulfilment follows a linear progression. Indeed, many, if not all, of its images tell the same story from different perspectives. At one time, the focus of a vision will be the suffering of persecuted believers. At another time, it will center on God's dealings with the persecutors. At yet another, it will show the glory that is resident within the destiny and nature of the church despite the conflict it is engaged in. And then it will reveal the jealous wrath of God against injustice. Throughout every scene, the victory and authority, the majesty and mystery, of the all-conquering, sovereign Christ trumpets its message to the reader: "Behold, I am coming quickly, and My reward is with Me, to give to everyone according to his work."[4]

- Because John most definitely understood the hundreds of Old Testament references and allusions that are contained within his writing, we can confidently say that he knew exactly what he was writing about. He was not, as many mistakenly believe, looking at a kind of video that showed events of a distant future, depicting sciences and technologies that he had no way of comprehending. To him, his message was straightforward and obvious, though clothed in the images of the Old Testament. Because he wrote in a genre foreign to our own day, I have

---

resurrections at the beginning and end of the millennium in Revelation 20. This is such a key element of popular Eschatology, that I will devote a considerable section to it in chapter 6, *When Christ Rules the World*.

4. Revelation 22:12.

found it helpful to compare his work with a close counterpart to a genre of our own times that you probably are familiar with. Imagine, if you will, someone writing a fantasy novel or fantasy screenplay. Imagine they had a theological agenda that lay under the telling of that story. It is likely that you have already read something like this in C. S. Lewis's *Chronicles of Narnia*. These Chronicles are a series of fantasies, but they reveal many of Lewis's views on theology and the Christian life. You can read the books purely as novels and they will just be interesting stories. Or you can look for Lewis's theological agenda and they become fascinating sermons hidden within the fantasy itself. That is an instructive illustration for how to read the Revelation. View it as a theologically-charged, fantasy drama. You will be surprised with what you find hidden between the lines of the story as it unfolds.

With these as our guiding principles, let us look at the book as a whole. I am not going to write a verse by verse commentary on the Revelation. That is not my purpose. In this chapter, I will introduce you to the literary structure of the book. You will find it both fascinating and instructive, and it will set you on the path for being able to interpret the images of the book yourself. Of course, some of these images regularly feature in popular teaching of Eschatology. I will definitely open those up to you in detail throughout the rest of this book.

IT IS THE REVELATION OF JESUS CHRIST

> The Revelation of Jesus Christ, which God gave Him to show His servants—things which must shortly take place. And He sent and signified it by His angel to His servant John. (Revelation 1:1)

So begins the last book of the New Testament, a book that is going to address the question: Where is God when Christians suffer for their faith? Yet before it looks baldly into the face and horrors of persecution, John makes sure that we start by looking into the face of the risen Savior.

It is the Revelation of Jesus Christ. You can read that introduction a couple of ways.

- It is the Revelation belonging to Jesus Christ, the Revelation that is his to unfold.
- Or it is the Revelation that shows us who Jesus really is, the Revelation of himself that he causes our eyes to see.

Both are appropriate ways to read the opening lines. And both are true. But note, it is not the Revelation of the end times! Though it will reveal *things which will take place after this*,[5] its focus is Jesus. As the reader turns each page of John's book, he or she will be confronted with all sorts of horror, trial, and persecution. But that is neither its focus nor its intent. Its purpose is to reveal Jesus to us in the very midst of that suffering.

> I, John, both your brother and companion in the tribulation and kingdom and patience of Jesus Christ, was on the island that is called Patmos for the word of God and for the testimony of Jesus Christ. (Revelation 1:9)

John wrote to the churches of Asia Minor[6] who were suffering under the same oppressive regime that had put him into exile on Patmos. He was their brother in the tribulation of Jesus Christ. Reflect on that for a moment. For all manner of suffering, there are promises of deliverance in the Bible for us to claim. Except persecution. Jesus has redeemed us from the curse of the fall, but in this one area, suffering for the sake of the gospel, there is no promise other than it is our honor to be counted among the vast number of those who have so suffered for their faith, our Savior included.[7]

---

5. Revelation 1:19.

6. What you see, write in a book and send it to the seven churches which are in Asia: to Ephesus, to Smyrna, to Pergamos, to Thyatira, to Sardis, to Philadelphia, and to Laodicea. (Revelation 1:11)

7. Blessed are those who are persecuted for righteousness' sake, for theirs is the kingdom of heaven. (Matthew 5:10)
For to you it has been granted on behalf of Christ, not only to believe on

The Revelation commences with a vision of the risen Christ holding the persecuted churches in his hand and dictating letters to them. For those same churches, it is an image that confirms their eternal safety and heavenly authority. It is Jesus who holds the keys of Hades and Death,[8] the One who truly lives.

You would think that any letters addressed to these suffering churches would be replete with words of comfort and consolation. But that is far from what we find. Chapters 2 and 3 are given over to the letters to the seven churches. Each follows the same pattern.

- Address: "To the angel[9] of the church of _____ write..."
- Author: "These things says he who (a description of the risen Christ that relates directly to the vision just shown us in chapter 1[10])..."
- Commendation: "I know your works..."
- Discommendation followed by injunction: "Nevertheless I have this against you..."[11]
- Conclusion: "He who has an ear, let him hear what the Spirit says to the churches." Although each letter is specific to the church it addresses, there is a message the Spirit is saying through it to all churches.

Him, but also to suffer for His sake. (Philippians 1:29).

8. Revelation 1:18.

9. The word *angel* comes from the Greek word *aggelos* (the *gg* in New Testament Greek is pronounced as *ng*), meaning *messenger*. It does not always refer to what we, in English, would call an angel. It can simply refer to any messenger. Commentators rightly take the usage in the seven letters as referring to the leader, or leadership team, of the particular church.

10. Ephesus (Revelation 2:1 cf Revelation 1:13, 16); Smyrna (Revelation 2:8 cf Revelation 1:11, 18); Pergamos (Revelation 2:12 cf Revelation 1:16); Thyatira (Revelation 2:18 cf Revelation 1:14); Sardis (Revelation 3:1 cf Revelation 1:16; 4:5); Philadelphia (Revelation 3:7 cf Revelation 1:18); Laodicea (Revelation 3:14 cf Revelation 1:8).

11. Two of the churches, Smyrna and Philadelphia, do not have any form of rebuke, only commendation.

- Promise: "To him who overcomes . . ." The promise that follows is taken from images that appear in the end of the Revelation.[12]

Each letter begins with an aspect of the vision of the Risen Christ from Revelation 1 and closes with allusions to the end of the Revelation.[13] So we note the following . . .

- John expects that his readers will read and re-read his book. The very first time anyone reads Revelation 2 and 3, the promises to those who overcome will make little sense. It is only as the reader comprehends the end of the book that they will understand what the Spirit is saying at the beginning of the book.
- The letters to the seven churches, which contain the Spirit's words to all churches, are bracketed by the revelation of the risen Christ and of his glorious Bride. We cannot hear what the Spirit is saying to us in today's world if we do not have a proper view of Christ or his Bride, the church.
- In many ways, the Spirit is talking to churches of all times throughout the Revelation. We therefore are instructed by the seven letters that those two revelations—the risen Christ and the glorious Bride—are significant to the book as a whole. They are the brackets, the bookends that hold the work together, that begin and end it. Our understanding of the visions within the Revelation's pages must draw from the revelation of the risen Christ or build towards the revelation of the glory of the church.

---

12. Ephesus (Revelation 2:7 cf Revelation 22:2, 14); Smyrna (Revelation 2:11 cf Revelation 20:14); Pergamos (Revelation 2:17 cf Revelation 19:12); Thyatira (Revelation 2:26–27 cf Revelation 19:15); Sardis (Revelation 3:5 cf Revelation 20:12); Philadelphia (Revelation 3:12 cf Revelation 21:2, 22:4); Laodicea (Revelation 3:21 cf Revelation 22:3).

13. In particular, the closing vision of the Revelation is a wonderful vision of the church, the Bride of the Lamb.

The Lost Message of the End Times

HEAR WHAT THE SPIRIT IS SAYING

A popular teaching in modern Christianity is that the letters to the churches of Revelation 2 and 3 refer to specific ages in the gospel era. There is little warrant for this, however. The entirety of John's Revelation was addressed to all seven churches.

> John, to the seven churches which are in Asia. (Revelation 1:4)

> I was in the Spirit on the Lord's Day, and I heard behind me a loud voice, as of a trumpet, saying, "I am the Alpha and the Omega, the First and the Last," and, "What you see, write in a book and send it to the seven churches which are in Asia: to Ephesus, to Smyrna, to Pergamos, to Thyatira, to Sardis, to Philadelphia, and to Laodicea." (Revelation 1:10–11)

It is obvious, then, that John believed the whole book was for all seven, and not to be broken up in piecemeal fashion. Because the Revelation is written to the churches both individually and collectively, its message is applicable in the same manner. With the words, "He who has an ear to hear, let him hear what the Spirit says to the churches," we are given instruction as to the purpose of the Revelation as a whole.

What, then, is the Spirit saying to the churches, as specifically highlighted in the seven letters to the seven churches?

- The message to Ephesus is to keep your relationship with Christ fresh. Remember your first love.
- The message to Smyrna is to remain faithful to Christ, despite hardship.
- The message to Pergamos is to hold uncompromisingly to the gospel.
- The message to Thyatira is twofold. For those who are complacent, Christ is holy and will not suffer blemishes in his Bride. To the rest, it is an encouragement to hold onto sound teaching.

- The message to Sardis is to avoid heartless religion.
- The message to Philadelphia is a promise of divine help for those who press toward the mark even though they are weary.
- The message to Laodicea is a warning against halting halfway between Christ and the world.

This is what the Spirit is saying to the churches. Put simply, the Spirit, throughout the Revelation, is saying one thing: Love Jesus and follow him with all your heart despite the cost. And he is still saying it today. It is the central message of the Revelation.

SETTING THE SCENE

When you are shown how the Revelation is constructed, it will help you know how to read and discern its message. If you can, imagine yourself at the end of the first century, sitting in a theatre. Around you are seated persecuted Christians from all the churches in the district you come from. The author, playing the part of the risen Christ, stands on the stage with the principal actor, John. He directs the principal actor to write letters to the churches that are represented by you, the audience. After dictating those letters, which you, the audience, hear, the curtain rolls back. The Prophetic Drama, set to reveal where God is in the midst of the seeming global persecution that you are suffering, begins . . .

Revelation 4 and 5 sets the scene for the prophecy as a whole. And it is not what you expect! Instead of conflict, there is praise. A glorious scene of the majesty and splendor of heaven, and the worthiness of the Lamb to take the scroll of your destiny in his hand.

Persecution, so dreadful on earth, cannot assail heaven, the home of your true identity. All is well. The drama will unfold before you as it will—you will be confronted by dragons and beasts and war and death—but all is well.

RHETORICAL FEATURES

The general consensus amongst many of today's teachers of popular Eschatology is that John saw things that he had never seen before. In this way, they seek to comprehend the often bizarre imagery of his writing. For example, the locusts of Revelation 9:9–10, with their breastplates of iron and stinging, scorpion-like tails, could merely be a first century man's attempts to describe twenty-first century military helicopters. Because so much teaching has fallen along those faulty exegetical lines, modern readers are predisposed to read the Revelation as a mysterious panorama of futuristic prophecy. This is far from John's intention.

Common to writers of his time, indeed common to writers of all time, rhetorical markers indicate definite patterns of thought that reveal John's intention in the Revelation. He knew exactly what he was writing and why he was writing it. Once the modern reader, schooled most likely in Dispensationalist Eschatology, takes off the colored lenses they have been taught to read the Revelation through, they will immediately become aware of many of the deliberate rhetorical devices that John employed.

RHETORICAL REPETITION: TESTIMONY AND MARTYRS

I will keep bringing you back to one important truth: the Revelation was written during a time of State-sanctioned persecution of the early church. Seven specific churches were addressed in the prophecy. All of these suffered intensely at that time. An important repetition features in John's choice of words, although unfortunately, it can get missed in English translations. So let me give you a brief study of four Greek words.

The first is the feminine noun, *marturia*, translated in the NKJV as *testimony*.[14] It is used of a formal testimony provided by a witness at a judicial hearing and is frequently used in the Revelation.[15]

The second is the masculine noun, *martus*. In its simplest sense, it means *witness*, either in a judicial setting or simply in the historical sense of someone who witnessed a notable event. Importantly for us, it was also used of someone who had been violently killed or executed because of the testimony they bore witness to. From *martus* comes our English word *martyr*.[16]

The third is the neuter noun, *marturion*. It was a word used of evidence brought forward in a court case, that which proved a matter.[17]

Finally, the verb *martureo*, meaning *to testify*, which occurs only three times in the Revelation, at the beginning (Revelation 1:2) and end (Revelation 22:16, 20) of the book. You could almost take this verb, *martureo*, then, to be a literary bookend that holds the whole work together.

As you can see, all four words are related, and if you look at the references in the footnotes, you will see how regularly they appear

14. I cannot determine why, but the NKJV translators rendered the phrase in Revelation 20:4 as *their witness to Jesus* when they elsewhere translate it as *the testimony of Jesus*.

15. John bore witness to the *testimony of Jesus Christ* (Revelation 1:2); he was on the Isle of Patmos for that same *testimony of Jesus Christ* (Revelation 1:9); the saints had been slain because of the *testimony which they held* (Revelation 6:9); the two witnesses were killed after they finished *their testimony* (Revelation 11:7); the saints overcame the devil by the *word of their testimony* (Revelation 12:11); the dragon was enraged with the woman's offspring who have *the testimony of Jesus Christ* (Revelation 12:17); the angel said that John's brothers have *the testimony of Jesus* (Revelation 19:10); the spirit of prophecy is *the testimony of Jesus* (Revelation 19:10); the first resurrection was of those who were beheaded for *the testimony of Jesus* (literal translation of Revelation 20:4).

16. Jesus is called *the faithful witness* (Revelation 1:5); Christ identified Antipas as *My faithful martyr* (Revelation 2:13); Jesus is called *the Amen, the Faithful and True Witness* (Revelation 3:14); power was given to Christ's *two witnesses* (Revelation 11:3); the woman was drunk on the *blood of the martyrs* (Revelation 17:6).

17. Though it occurs elsewhere in the New Testament, the word only appears once in the Revelation, in the expression "the tabernacle of the testimony" (Revelation 15:5).

in the Revelation. Now put that within the context of writing to a group of churches that have been caught up in a period of intense persecution. Antipas, the faithful martyr of Revelation 2:13, was someone they knew, one of their own number who had given his life for his faith in the testimony of Jesus. Throughout the Revelation, John both affirms his audience's witness in the face of this suffering and underlines the fact that, in that very persecution, they are identifying with their Savior. More to the point, however, despite Jesus suffering cruel torture and death at the hands of wicked men, it was the pathway for resurrection.[18]

RHETORICAL REPETITION: I SAW AND I HEARD

> Now I, John, saw and heard these things. And when I heard and saw,[19] I fell down to worship before the feet of the angel who showed me these things. (Revelation 22:8)

The Revelation is broken into four main sections, or Acts within the Prophetic Drama, which I will shortly show you. Within these larger portions of the work, many times you will come across expressions similar to "After this I saw" or "Then I heard." John employs this to break each Act into smaller scenes.

RHETORICAL REPETITION: LIGHTNINGS AND THUNDERS AND VOICES

A powerful repetition builds to a crescendo as you make your way through the Revelation. It starts with a door standing open in heaven.

---

18. See for instance, the raising of the two witnesses in Revelation 11:7–11.

19. I note the mirrored *saw and heard/heard and saw*. I make no explanation for why John did that, but I draw your attention to it for a reason. Middle Eastern authors (not just Biblical) employ a rhetorical device that scholars call a Chiasm. It is when a story reflects, as in a mirror, about a central moment of the story. Whenever you see the elements of a story repeating in reverse order to how they were first presented, look for the single thought/statement/line that lies in the middle of the mirror. It is usually the main point of the story.

> After these things I looked, and behold, a door standing open in heaven ... And from the throne proceeded lightnings, thunderings, and voices. (Revelation 4:5)

In the Old Testament, lightning and thunder are regularly associated with the throne of the Lord in heaven, a display of his majestic glory.[20] But they also appear throughout the narrative of the Old Testament where God fights on behalf of his people. Perhaps already we have learned enough about the purpose of the Revelation to know that John will use these images in terms of God fighting on behalf of his persecuted saints, but let me show you clearly that this is, indeed, his intention.

Concerning the verse just quoted, Revelation 4:5, if it was the only of its sort in John's writing, there would be nothing much to discuss. But watch what happens as the Revelation unfolds.

> Then the angel took the censer, filled it with fire from the altar, and threw it to the earth. And there were noises, thunderings, lightnings, and an earthquake. (Revelation 8:5)

Take particular note of the ordering of the three elements that were first introduced to us in Revelation 4:5. There, it was lightnings, thunderings, and voices. Now, in Revelation 8:5, the order is reversed—noises,[21] thunderings, and lightnings. But it builds. An earthquake is added.

---

20. Examples are many, but a beautiful one, tying together voices, thunders and lightnings, is found in Job 37:1–5. "At this also my heart trembles, and leaps from its place. Hear attentively the thunder of His voice, and the rumbling that comes from His mouth. He sends it forth under the whole heaven, His lightning to the ends of the earth. After it a voice roars; He thunders with His majestic voice, and He does not restrain them when His voice is heard. God thunders marvelously with His voice; He does great things which we cannot comprehend."

21. The NKJV uses the word *noises*, and for that you would expect that the translators are dealing with a different Greek word to that used previously in Revelation 4:5, which had *voices*. This is not the case, however. The same word is used in both texts. The translators have probably gone with *voices* in Revelation 4:5 because they are associated with the throne of God, about which are the four living creatures, the twenty-four elders and the seven spirits of God. The Greek word itself can truly be translated as *noises* but it is most commonly

> Then the temple of God was opened in heaven, and the ark of His covenant was seen in His temple. And there were lightnings, noises, thunderings, an earthquake, and great hail. (Revelation 11:19)

Once more, the order of the first three elements is altered, and this time great hail is added to the earthquake. The tension is growing. We are building to a climax.

> And there were noises and thunderings and lightnings;[22] and there was a great earthquake, such a mighty and great earthquake as had not occurred since men were on the earth . . . Then every island fled away, and the mountains were not found. And great hail from heaven fell upon men, each hailstone about the weight of a talent. (Revelation 16:18, 21)

The order of the initial three, yet again, is manipulated, but now the earthquake is a great earthquake, so great as has never been witnessed before, and each hailstone is massive, around one hundred pounds.

All this is used by John for dramatic effect. Taken together, we feel the growing sense of impending judgment. With the escalation of earthquakes and hailstorms, we are not reminded of Old Testament visions of God's majestic throne, but rather, of the many judgments of God against his enemies.[23]

As the drama unfolds, then, John is leading his persecuted audience by the hand. Judgment is coming. The Lord will avenge

---

associated with speech. For that reason, *voices* is, in my opinion, a better choice and should feature throughout the Revelation.

22. This is a word for word translation. In all three previous repetitions of this expression, the translators have dropped the *and* in favour of a comma. This makes it read better for sure, but the reader is unaware as to how much of a repetition the expression really is.

23. The plagues against Egypt are regularly alluded to in the Revelation. Consider Exodus 9:23. "And Moses stretched out his rod toward heaven; and the Lord sent thunder and hail, and fire darted to the ground. And the Lord rained hail on the land of Egypt. So there was hail, and fire mingled with the hail, so very heavy that there was none like it in all the land of Egypt since it became a nation." This is just one example, of course. In the historical narrative of Israel, earthquakes and hail appear regularly against God's enemies.

his own. Individual horrifying scenes within the drama, with their dragons and beasts and harlots, will not be the end of the story. Hold fast. Vindication is at hand.

RHETORICAL REPETITION: DOORS OPENED

To my mind, this is the most important of the repetitions that feature in John's prophecy. Four times we are confronted with a heavenly door standing open. Three of these will be seen in conjunction with one of the cascading visions of lightnings, thunders, and noises. On each occasion, it is relatively simple to show that they mark the beginning of a whole new section in the Revelation. They are so important, in fact, that I will look at each in turn.

A DOOR STANDING OPEN IN HEAVEN

> After these things I looked, and behold, a door standing open in heaven. (Revelation 4:1)

This is akin to the first Act of the Prophetic Drama, following its Introduction (chapters 1 to 3). With the open door in heaven (Revelation 4:1), we are introduced to the Lion of the tribe of Judah, the Root of David, who has prevailed to open the scroll of man's destiny and loose its seven seals. The seven seals are opened (Revelation 6:1—8:1), and each depicts the unfolding crisis the persecuted churches were suffering.

Pay attention to how the narrative of the seven seals unfolds. The first six are opened one after the other (Revelation 6:1–17),[24] yet before the seventh is opened, there is an interlude in which the saints are sealed (Revelation 7:1–17). In this, Jesus is encouraging his suffering people that they have been especially marked. They are not forgotten but are playing a part in a much bigger picture.

---

24. An interesting observation is that the first four seals are dealt with quickly in the narrative, with more attention given to seals five and six. This same pattern will be repeated shortly with the sounding of the trumpets in Revelation 8.

With the opening of the seventh seal, there was silence in heaven (Revelation 8:1). Reader pay attention: stop and ponder what you have just witnessed in the opening of the scrolls. It is John's version of the Psalmist's *Selah*.

With the half hour silence in heaven, we are then introduced to the second half of this first Act of the Prophetic Drama. Seven angels with seven trumpets. As with the opening of the seven seals, the narrative looks at the sounding of each trumpet.[25] And as with the seals, the sounding of the first six trumpets (Revelation 8:6–9:21) is followed by an interlude (Revelation 10:1—11:14). This interlude depicts the gospel being preached[26] and the resurrection power and authority of the witnessing church.[27]

When the seventh seal was opened, there was silence in heaven. Now, when the seventh trumpet is sounded, there are loud voices of praise in heaven (Revelation 11:15-18). Reader follow suit.

This first Act, then, is broken into three main sections:

- The vision of the throne, those around the throne, and the One who sat on the throne (Revelation 4:1—5:14)
- The opening of the seven seals and the sealing on the foreheads of the servants of God (Revelation 6:1—8:6)
- The sounding of the seven trumpets and the preaching of the gospel with the ministry of the two witnesses (Revelation 8:7—11:18)

---

25. You will notice that before the first of the seven trumpets is sounded, we have one of the repetitions we studied earlier—noises, thunderings, lightnings, and an earthquake (Revelation 8:5).

26. To help you see this, compare the little book that John was to eat (Revelation 10:9-11). It is meant to remind us of the call on two of the major prophets, Jeremiah 15:16 and Ezekiel 2:10; 3:3.

27. Because the two witnesses of Revelation 11 are so widely misunderstood in popular Eschatology, we will discuss this passage more fully in chapter 8, *Prophetic Times*.

THE TEMPLE OF GOD OPENED

> Then the temple of God was opened in heaven, and the ark of His covenant was seen in His temple. And there were lightnings, noises, thunderings, an earthquake, and great hail. (Revelation 11:19)

With the opening of the temple of God in heaven, the Second Act of the Prophetic Drama begins. Our attention is drawn to a great sign, a woman in conflict with a dragon (Revelation 12:1-17). This will be the first of seven major scenes before we come to the next door opening. In Act One, where a door was open in heaven, we were given an overview of God at work in the events of our world. Now, in Act Two, where the temple of God in heaven is now open, we dive deeper to understand the undercurrents of the unholy forces that seek to wreak havoc on God and his people.[28]

The seven scenes of Act Two are:

- The woman and dragon in conflict (Revelation 12:1-17)
- The beast from the sea (Revelation 13:1-10)
- The beast from the earth (Revelation 13:11-18)
- The Lamb and the 144,000 (Revelation 14:1-5)[29]
- Three angels proclaiming impending judgment (Revelation 14:6-13)
- The double harvest (Revelation 14:14-20)

---

28. I struggle to know how deep to dive into each of these scenes. They are fascinating, but it is not my intention to write a commentary on the Revelation. Hopefully, by the time you have finished studying this book, I will have guided you well enough for you to be able to discover for yourself how easily the images can be understood when studied devotionally. My only injunction to you is this: do it devotionally, not academically. Do not go to the commentators for answers—many of the popular ones right now follow a Dispensational framework, and we are not wearing their glasses. Use the principles you have learned from this book, and sit before the Lord yourself and write what you observe, devotionally, in his presence. It will be a rich and rewarding experience.

29. Notice that the dragon is seen from the sand (Revelation 13:1) while, in contrast, the Lamb stands on the mountain of Zion (Revelation 14:1).

- Introduction of the seven angels with the last plagues (Revelation 15:1–4)[30]

THE TEMPLE OF THE TABERNACLE OF THE TESTIMONY WAS OPENED

> After these things I looked, and behold, the temple of the tabernacle of the testimony in heaven was opened. (Revelation 15:5)

Act Three of the Prophetic Drama begins with the temple of the tabernacle of the testimony opening. We are coming to the dramatic climax. Act One merely had a door open. In Act Two, the temple of God was open. Now in Act Three, it is the temple of the tabernacle[31] of the testimony.[32] In this powerful Act, we see the beginning of God's vindication of his persecuted saints. It commences with the seven angels, introduced in the previous Act, pouring out their bowls of God's wrath on the earth.[33] God has not forgotten the unjust suffering of his persecuted children.

> And I heard the angel of the waters saying: "You are righteous, O Lord, the One who is and who was and who is to be, because You have judged these things. For they have shed the blood of saints and prophets, and You have given them blood to drink. For it is their just due." (Revelation 16:5–6)

---

30. With the reference to *another sign* in Revelation 15:1, John effectively has bound together these images that form what I am calling the Second Act of the Prophetic Drama, which started with the *great sign* of Revelation 12:1.

31. It is an interesting expression ... the temple of the tabernacle. The word *tabernacle* means *tent*. In the Old Testament, the Israelites gathered around the tabernacle that Moses had instructed them to build. Later, in the time of King Solomon, the tent was replaced with a building, the temple. I will leave you to ponder the significance of joining the two in the one expression, *the temple of the tabernacle of the testimony*.

32. The testimony, as we have seen, is a significant repetition.

33. Revelation 16:1–17.

The wrath of God is not a popular preaching topic in our modern world. In our efforts to emphasize the once almost forgotten truths of his goodness and kindness, his joy and his singing over us, we have wandered away from the sobering, even frightening, side of his majesty. Two truths stand equally within the nature of God—mercy and justice. In our presentation of the gospel, we understand that people need mercy. But is it possible that in our desire to preach mercy for the guilty, we have neglected the need for justice for the innocent? The abuser needs to know that God is merciful, but the abused needs to know that God is just. Vengeance is a part of the holy jealousy that God has for his people. And this is where wrath finds its perfect home. It is not for us to wreak vengeance on our abusers—we would never do that with purity; it would fuel an unholy side of our fleshly nature. But the desire for vengeance, for vindication, for innocence to be upheld and defended, is a righteous desire.

> Beloved, do not avenge yourselves, but rather give place to wrath; for it is written, "Vengeance is Mine, I will repay," says the Lord. (Romans 12:19)

With the pouring out of the bowls of God's wrath, John's original readers, suffering unjustly as they were under brutal persecution, would most definitely discover that God had not forgotten them. He is the defender of the weak and the upholder of their blood-bought righteousness.

The ultimate depiction of God's wrath on behalf of his people is found in the juxtaposition of the destruction of "Babylon the Great, the Mother of Harlots and of the Abominations of the Earth"[34] with the announcement of the marriage supper of the Lamb and the readiness of his Bride.[35]

The harlot is easy to identify, particularly for a persecuted Christian of the first century. Babylon was one of the great kingdoms of the Old Testament period, responsible for the deportation and exile of the Jews that stretched throughout the sixth century BC. For John's original audience, the name evoked the pride of the nations

---

34. Revelation 17:5.
35. Revelation 19:7–9.

that worked in opposition to God's purposes for his people. They would quickly have seen the embodiment of this in the contemporary Roman world.[36] Added to this, through the mouths of the prophets of the Old Testament, the covenant making God, YHWH, regularly likened Israel's unfaithfulness to playing the harlot. Pursuing other gods was, to him, the same as seeking other lovers.

Babylon the Great seduces people away from God and brings the family of believers into bondage. In essence, she is the world,[37] the antithesis of the Kingdom; Babylon, the antithesis of Jerusalem.

In contrast to the certain doom that awaits Babylon, the persecuted church is shown to be a Bride, ready for her wedding to her Groom. The message to those suffering under the demonic persecution of that time, indeed of any time, is an important one to hear. We need a revelation of who we are in Christ. Collectively. We are his glorious Bride. His affections are for us. His desire is for us. His love is constant, and he is quick to defend us.

In seven scenes, Act Three describes the downfall of Babylon:

- The seven bowls of God's wrath (Revelation 16:1–17)
- Babylon, the harlot (Revelation 17:1–5)
- The mystery of Babylon explained (Revelation 17:6–18)
- The fall of Babylon proclaimed (Revelation 18:1–3)
- The fall of Babylon detailed (Revelation 18:4–24)
- The loud praises in heaven (Revelation 19:1–5)
- Announcement of the marriage of the Lamb (Revelation 19:6–10)

HEAVEN ITSELF OPENED

Now I saw heaven opened, and behold, a white horse. And He who sat on him was called Faithful and True,

---

36. Compare with Peter's veiled reference to Rome in 1 Peter 5:13.
37. 1 John 2:15.

and in righteousness He judges and makes war. (Revelation 19:11)

Act Four of the Prophetic Drama begins with heaven itself open. And with it, we are drawn to a powerful image of the risen Christ, seated on a white horse, in righteousness judging and making war. For the suffering, persecuted Christian of the turn of the first century, this is a majestic introduction to the climax of John's prophecy. In this last Act, we see the ultimate destruction of the Beast, the False Prophet, the Dragon, the kings of the earth who waged war against Christ's followers, and the final judgment of the living and the dead.[38]

The Act closes with a stunning image of the glory of the church, the New Jerusalem, the Bride of the Lamb, who descends from her royal, heavenly seat of privilege in preparation for her marriage.[39] These two glorious pictures, the Rider on the white horse and the Holy City descending from heaven, form bookends around seven scenes of the end of the persecution of those who hold the testimony of Jesus.

Each scene has the same introduction: "And I saw . . ." They depict, in panoramic fashion, God's wonderful plan of salvation. As is true of the whole Revelation, the scenes are not meant to be understood in chronological order. They are largely true of all time, and speak powerfully to all believers, particularly those who, like John's original audience, suffer under intense persecution because of their faith.

The seven scenes of Act Four with its two bookends are:

- Bookend: The Rider on the White Horse (Revelation 19:11–16)
- Announcement of judgment (Revelation 19:17–18)
- The beast and false prophet cast into the lake of fire (Revelation 19:19–21)
- The devil cast into the bottomless pit (Revelation 20:1–3)

---

38. We will look in greater detail at Revelation 20 in chapter 6, *When Christ Rules the World*, because it contains some famous images surrounding the resurrection of the dead that are greatly misunderstood by modern believers.

39. Revelation 21:2—22:5.

- The thousand years (Revelation 20:4–10)[40]
- The great white throne (Revelation 20:11)
- Judgment Day (Revelation 20:12)
- New heavens and new earth (Revelation 21:1)
- Bookend: The holy city, the new Jerusalem, the bride of the Lamb (Revelation 21:2—22:5)

I have probably said enough about this Act to point you in the right direction for your personal devotional studies, but first let me draw attention to a couple of the details of the powerful bookends of this portion of the Prophetic Drama.

> Now I saw heaven opened, and behold, a white horse. And He who sat on him was called Faithful and True, and in righteousness He judges and makes war. (Revelation 19:11)

Behold! A white horse and he who sat on it. John, in the words that follow, paints a powerful and majestic portrayal of Christ in all his matchless glory. His eyes are like flames. He is crowned with many crowns. His robe is drenched in blood. His armies follow him, clothed in white linen and riding white horses like their Lord. He has a sharp sword in his mouth that strikes the nations and rules them with an iron rod.[41] Ultimately, he treads out the winepress of the fierceness and wrath of Almighty God.

---

40. In Revelation 20:4, many translations include the words *"Then I saw"* when referring to the souls of those who had been beheaded. This is not literal to the Greek language of John's Revelation which simply reads "And I saw thrones and they sat on them and judgment was committed to them and the souls of those who had been beheaded for the testimony of Jesus."

41. The original language of this is incredible. The NKJV translates Revelation 19:15 as "And he himself will rule them with a rod of iron." It is an allusion to the Messianic exhortation of Psalm 2:9, "You shall break them with a rod of iron; You shall dash them to pieces like a potter's vessel." And that is why the translators use the word *rule* in Revelation 19:15. It will surprise you to learn that the Greek word that John used in this verse is the verb *to shepherd*. "And he himself will shepherd them with a rod of iron." There is a wonderful devotional trail to follow there if you are willing. Why *shepherd*? And why link the *rod of iron* to it?

This is fuel for an eternity of praise and adoration. But see how John paints the picture of us, Christ's followers. We are clothed in righteousness, white linen, because he is clothed in a robe drenched in his own blood. We are his armies, but we are not armies engaged in bloody war. Our all-conquering Captain rules with the Word of his mouth.

We are immediately reminded of the familiar Old Testament expression, the LORD of Hosts. Some modern translations, when translating the Hebrew *YHWH Tzevaot*, render it LORD Almighty, but to my mind, this weakens the force of the expression. The popular Message Translation uses the expression God-of-the-Angel-Armies. And this also misses the point. The hosts of heaven are the blood-bought, new-creation people of God, seated now in heavenly places in Christ. Heaven's armies are us, the redeemed, the Old and New Covenant people together, Jew and Gentile alike.

And his Name is given significance in this passage.[42] He is called Faith-filled[43] and True.[44] In that names hold significance for John in this scene, it is of interest that the first two are not identified as names per se, but rather what Christ is called. In our relationship with him, we have found him to be full of faith and true. It is we who have given him these names because it is only by personal experience that we can know him as such.

---

42. As is common throughout both Old and New Testaments, names are often prophetic declarations of the nature, character or promises of the person so named. These are most powerful when they relate to the Person of God himself, as we see here in Revelation 19:11–16.

43. English translations invariably render the Greek adjective, *pistos*, as *faithful*. It is the adjectival form of the Greek noun, *pistis*—*faith*. Personally, I do not believe that *faithful* adequately translates the adjectival form of *faith* as it maybe once did when the Bible was first brought into the English language. When modern Christians hear the word *faithful*, we hear *steadfast*—dependable, reliable, consistent, perseverant. These are all important qualities, for sure, but they do not carry the power and force of the word *faith*, which believes the impossible and calls those things that are not as though they were. *Faith-filled* is a better adjective, in my opinion, and one that shows an aspect of our Savior in Revelation 19:11 that is important for us to see. He is a Believer! He calls us to a life of faith because that best reflects his own life!

44. Revelation 19:11.

He has a Name written that no one knows except himself.[45] This emphatically declares that there are aspects of his nature that are not revealed to us. He is far more glorious than even his blood-washed armies, riding on white horses like his, are aware.

His Name is the Word of God,[46] the one who was from the beginning.[47]

And his Name is King of kings and Lord of lords.[48] This identifies him as King and Lord over the rulers and masters of this world. What a powerful assertion to those who are suffering under the unjust abuse of worldly kings and lords! But it is doubly true that Christ is our King and our Lord. By calling him King of kings and Lord of lords, we are struck with the revelation of the royal, priestly authority of those who follow him. We are kings and lords under our great Sovereign!

What an image for the first of the bookends of this fourth and final Act of the Prophetic Drama. And it closes with an equally dramatic bookend! A compelling image of the Holy City, the Bride of Christ, the church.

Remember that the Revelation was first written to the persecuted churches of Asia Minor. The prophecy has reached its climax. All is well. God is in charge. Jesus is victorious. The church is majestic and significant. Despite the atrocities that believers may face, their outward display of weakness, and the brutal suffering they may endure, the church is glorious. God is with us and wipes away the tears of our suffering.[49] We are clothed with the very glory of God.[50] Even though there may be periods when the church is persecuted, its destiny is to lead the nations who will walk in its

---

45. Revelation 19:12.

46. Revelation 19:13.

47. In the beginning was the Word, and the Word was with God, and the Word was God. He was in the beginning with God. All things were made through Him, and without Him nothing was made that was made. (John 1:1–3)

48. Revelation 19:16.

49. Revelation 21:3–4.

50. Revelation 21:11.

light and bring glory and honor to it.[51] Within the church is a river that is to bring healing to the nations.[52]

What a destiny! And at the same time, what a challenge to a persecuted church; its oppressors need healing that only we can bring to them! This is perhaps one of the most radical aspects of the gospel. Our persecutors are not our enemies, they are victims of the demonic forces that enslave them. Like our Savior, we pray for them: "Lord, forgive them, for they do not know what they are doing."

This image of the Bride is not awaiting some far-off fulfilment. It is true right now. The Spirit of prophecy, through John's Revelation, wants us to capture a revelation of who we are in Christ. Right now! We are kings and priests. We are rulers. We are citizens of heaven. The heavenly city. We bring healing to the nations. This is a powerful revelation once you see it. We are not history makers. We are future shapers! We bring hope and healing and freedom and justice. You might see yourself as weak but look! You are seated on a white horse like Jesus. You are clothed in his righteousness. You might be weak, but he is riding before you!

REDEMPTION IN ACTION

And so the Revelation concludes. It is the story of redemption in action and of the time-altering glory resident within the gathering of believers, those made righteous by the blood of Christ. In its pages we see the revelation, not of the end time, but of all time.

> Blessed is he who reads and those who hear the words of this prophecy, and keep those things which are written in it; for the time is near. (Revelation 1:3)

> For I testify to everyone who hears the words of the prophecy of this book: If anyone adds to these things, God will add to him the plagues that are written in this book; and if anyone takes away from the words of the

---

51. Revelation 21:24–26.
52. Revelation 22:1–2.

book of this prophecy, God shall take away his part from the Book of Life, from the holy city, and from the things which are written in this book. (Revelation 22:18–19)

In this chapter, we have merely scratched the surface of the Revelation, but I trust that by now, you have seen what an incredibly important book it is. And hopefully, I have given you the tools that will help you explore its core message and the encouragement it will give you whenever your world might be assailed by fear, uncertainty, or confusion.

The amazing Revelation concludes with Christ's threefold declaration . . .

"Behold, I am coming quickly!" (Revelation 22:7)

"And behold, I am coming quickly!" (Revelation 22:12)

"Surely I am coming quickly." (Revelation 22:20)

And as the curtains come down on the Prophetic Drama, we reply with John, "Amen. Even so, come, Lord Jesus!" (Revelation 22:20)

5

The War of Armageddon

THE GREAT TRIBULATION, ARMAGEDDON, Gog and Magog—these are themes that feature heavily in teachings about the Second Coming. They are seldom understood, however, causing many Christians to expect great trials and hardship to fall on the world in the lead up to Jesus' return. As bad things happen, you can all but hear some people's excitement, as if the last trumpet is about to sound.[1] Tragically, they forget that when calamities fall, they do so on people that Jesus died for. There is something wrong when our Eschatology leads us to be happy when catastrophes strike. In this chapter, we will bring a proper perspective to these ominous and dark themes.

THE GREAT TRIBULATION

The popular Dispensational view of prophecy expects a terrible period of suffering, usually held to be seven years long, called the Great Tribulation, associated with the return of Christ.[2] We have already discussed it in relation to the Olivet Discourse in chapter 3, *Signs of the Times*. There we saw that Jesus' description of the great

---

1. 1 Thessalonians 4:16.

2. Proponents of Dispensationalism vary on how the return of Christ and the Great Tribulation work together. Some believe the church is raptured before the Tribulation, some in the middle of it, and some at the end.

tribulation referred to the suffering inflicted on Judea at the time of the first century Roman-Jewish war. But in this chapter, we will dig a little deeper.

Tribulation is the word the translators use to express a Greek noun that means *affliction, persecution, trouble.* It is a very graphic term, literally meaning *to be hard pressed* as when grapes are put in a winepress to extract their juice or when olives are crushed to extract their oil. Occurring frequently in the Greek New Testament, and not always translated as *tribulation,* there is nothing unique about the word in and of itself.

Ever since Jesus saw Satan fall like lightning out of heaven,[3] the church has been living alongside tribulation.[4] John, who wrote the Revelation, saw it this way when he introduced himself as "your brother and companion in the tribulation and kingdom and patience of Jesus Christ."[5] It can be difficult for Western Christians to accept this. Life in the West is relatively comfortable, and for the most part, we are free to exercise our faith in Christ. Yet this is not true for everyone in the world.

Of course, none of this is in contradiction to the popular views concerning the great tribulation. Everyone accepts that trial and persecution have marched hand in hand with the growth of the church over the centuries. But is there a final tribulation, a great one that eclipses them all?

To answer that, we will go to Revelation 7.

> Then one of the elders answered, saying to me, "Who are these arrayed in white robes, and where did they come from?" And I said to him, "Sir, you know." So he said to me, "These are the ones who come out of the great tribulation, and washed their robes and made them white in the blood of the Lamb. Therefore they are before the throne of God, and serve Him day and night in His temple. And He who sits on the throne will dwell among them. They shall neither hunger anymore nor thirst anymore; the sun shall not strike them, nor any heat; for the Lamb who is in

---

3. Luke 10:18.
4. See John 16:33; Acts 14:22.
5. Revelation 1:9.

the midst of the throne will shepherd them and lead them to living fountains of waters. And God will wipe away every tear from their eyes. (Revelation 7:13–17)

It is most definite that John's original audience saw themselves in these words. They were enduring great tribulation at the time of their reading of the Revelation and would have been greatly comforted and encouraged with the assertion that the Lamb leads them to fountains of living water and tenderly wipes away their tears. But surely, some may demand, this passage indicates something other than the persecution that has afflicted believers throughout history. It talks about those who came out of the great tribulation, not tribulation in general! For us, it all hinges on the use of that one word, *the*. Not just tribulation, but the tribulation.

Unfortunately, this is an example of the occasional difficulties scholars face when translating the New Testament into English. Our word *the* is called by grammarians, the definite article. We use it sparingly in English to distinguish a noun as being specific. For example, when I say, "A child ran onto a road," you have no idea what child or what road I am talking of. It could be any child on any road. But if I said, "The child ran onto the road," you would know from the context of our discussion which child and road I was referring to.

Hence, when the angel in Revelation 7:14 talks of the great tribulation, we assume he is referring to a specific tribulation, the great one. *The* tribulation. That is the way we use the definite article in English.

The trouble is, New Testament Greek, unlike English, is fluid with its use of the definite article. It uses it a lot, even when we would not. For example, Jesus Christ is regularly, though not always, written as, *the Jesus Christ*. That does not mean there are others; it is just the way of the Greek language. The definite article is often used when, in English, we would not. At other times, it does not use the article at all even when a specific noun is being referenced. John's opening sentence introducing his Revelation omits the definite article when referring to the *Revelation of Jesus Christ*. To top it off, at times the Greek text even uses the article for adjectives. Jesus Christ can appear as *the Jesus the Christ*. We see this in the case of Revelation 7:14 that we quoted above, which in Greek reads *the tribulation the great*. There is just no rigid uniformity regarding the Greek use of the definite article.

For the most part, this is no cause for alarm. The context almost always makes it strikingly easy to know when the English translation requires an *a*, a *the*, or no article at all. But just every now and then, the translators' theological beliefs influence their decision on what to do with the article. *Tribulation* is just such an example. If the translator believes there will be an end time tribulation, the Greek use of the definite article is important. If the translator believes tribulation may or may not heighten at the end before Jesus' return, the Greek use of the definite article is less significant. And if the translator believes that tribulation is ongoing for the duration of the history of the church, the use of the definite article is irrelevant. All of these conclusions would be in keeping with the original Greek writing.[6]

So what are we to make of it? Should we keep the definite article or not? Which should it be?

- "These are the ones who come out of the great tribulation, and washed their robes and made them white in the blood of the Lamb."

---

6. It is an interesting exercise to note the way the various translations handle the use of the definite article in relation to *great tribulation* in Revelation 7:14. The old translations (Authorized Version, Douay-Reims 1899 American Edition, 1599 Geneva Bible, and Wycliffe Bible) do not use the definite article—the ones clothed in white had come out of great tribulation. The new translations almost invariably use the definite article—the ones clothed in white had come out of *the* great tribulation. In fact, I could only find one modern translation—The Passion Translation—that does not use the definite article. None of this is because the older translations used inferior texts. They had access to the same Greek manuscript of Revelation 7:14 as the modern translators. The only difference is that, go back a hundred years or so and the dispensational view of prophecy (which believes strongly in an end time tribulation) was not a belief held amongst the theological community. And yet, that view is so widespread today that you can see its influence on all the modern translations of Revelation 7:14—apart from the Passion Translation.

- "These are the ones who come out of great tribulation, and washed their robes and made them white in the blood of the Lamb."

Because John's first century readers so clearly saw themselves in this picture, we need not be overly concerned by the use of the definite article. Ultimately, we will side with the bulk of commentators over the centuries who have not granted the definite article any weight.

Will there be a time of unprecedented terror before Jesus comes back? We reply that, in this life, there will always be tribulation.[7] However, there is no prophecy which predicts a cataclysmic persecution of believers befalling our world immediately prior to Christ's return. We need not fear the future; the Father is right now in the process of putting all Jesus' enemies under Christ's feet![8] There is a Kingdom for us to embrace, an identity as sons to accept, an authority to claim, and an inheritance to expect. And through it all, there may well be persecution. It is part of what it means to follow Christ.

THE TWO WITNESSES

We have previously seen in chapter 4, *Uncovering the Apocalypse*, how central the theme of tribulation and persecution is to the New Testament's prophetic book, the Revelation. It is overtly depicted in many of its scenes and visions. One that is prominent in a lot of popular teaching is the vision concerning two witnesses in Revelation 11. It is a powerful and liberating scene, especially for those

---

7. This is important when tribulation is understood in terms of persecution, not suffering in general. When someone suffers mentally or emotionally or physically, there are promises we seek to apply. We pray in faith. And so we should. Suffering is not a friend. But persecution is altogether different. We do not like it, but when it comes upon us, Jesus tells us to rejoice. Let me stress, though, we are talking about persecution, not suffering. There is a world of difference between the two. Jesus took upon himself our curse and all the suffering that attends it. But he did not redeem us from persecution. Refer John 16:33; 2 Timothy 3:12.

8. Hebrews 10:12–13.

Christians who, like John's original audience, face severe persecution for their faith in Jesus.

> Then I was given a reed like a measuring rod. And the angel stood, saying, "Rise and measure the temple of God, the altar, and those who worship there. But leave out the court which is outside the temple, and do not measure it, for it has been given to the Gentiles. And they will tread the holy city underfoot for forty-two months. (Revelation 11:1–2)

Keep in mind what we have already learned about the Revelation; it is not meant to be read literally. The temple is the New Testament church.[9] Measuring, from a cultural Jewish perspective, is either for destruction or preservation,[10] so here, in context, it speaks of God's preservation of his people. John was told, however, not to measure the courtyard. In this way, all humanity is contained within the image—believers (temple) and non-believers (courtyard). Non-believers hold dominance over the church, trampling the holy city for forty-two months.[11]

> And I will give power to my two witnesses, and they will prophesy one thousand two hundred and sixty days, clothed in sackcloth. These are the two olive trees and the two lampstands standing before the God of the earth. (Revelation 11:3–4)

With these words, John introduces us to the main characters of this scene. The two witnesses. I have heard some of the most remarkable beliefs surrounding these two. Teachers of Eschatology see the powers that are given to the two in this scene and immediately think of the prophet Elijah. And rightly so, he is definitely alluded to. But because Elijah did not die in the normal sense of that word, but was taken up to heaven directly in a whirlwind, it is

---

9. Refer 1 Corinthians 3:16; 2 Corinthians 6:16; Ephesians 2:20–22; 1 Peter 2:5.

10. Compare with 2 Samuel 8:2.

11. The forty-two months and also the one thousand two hundred and sixty days that follow in the next verse have particular significance, which we will discuss in chapter 8, *Prophetic Times*.

believed that he still has a role to play in the lead up to the return of Christ. That is, they expect Elijah to return to earth as one of the two witnesses.

This sounds remarkably like the error of the first century Jewish scribes, who taught that Elijah must come first.[12] That belief was a misunderstanding of one of Malachi's prophecies[13] and Jesus had to correct the mistake. He taught his disciples not to expect a literal fulfilment to Malachi's prophecy and showed that it had been fulfilled in the person of John the Baptist. We would do well to pay attention to how Jesus interprets prophecy. Nevertheless, many people read this scene of Revelation literally, and so expect Elijah to return before Christ.

I have heard a couple of candidates put forward for the second of the two witnesses—chiefly Enoch or Moses. Enoch, because like Elijah, he did not die but was raised directly to heaven.[14] And Moses, because like Elijah, he appeared with Christ on the mount of transfiguration.[15]

Although Moses is clearly alluded to in John's description of the two witnesses, which we will presently see, we are not meant to see two literal people. This is made apparent in the passage itself—John told us who the two witnesses are; the two olive trees and the two lampstands that stand before the God of the earth.

So who are the two olive trees? And who are the two lampstands? To answer that, we must go back to the book of Zechariah because John is leading us there.

> Then I answered and said to him, "What are these two olive trees—at the right of the lampstand and at its left?" And I further answered and said to him, "What are these two olive branches that drip into the receptacles of the two gold pipes from which the golden oil drains?" Then he answered me and said, "Do you not know what these are?" And I said, "No, my lord." So he said, "These are

---

12. See Matthew 17:10–13.
13. Malachi 4:5.
14. Genesis 5:24.
15. Matthew 17:2–3.

the two anointed ones, who stand beside the Lord of the whole earth." (Zechariah 4:11–14)

These anointed ones are clearly identified in the book of Zechariah. They were Joshua the high priest[16] and Zerubbabel the governor. I will explain.

> Hear, O Joshua, the high priest, you and your companions who sit before you, for they are a wondrous sign; for behold, I am bringing forth My Servant the BRANCH. (Zechariah 3:8)

Look at those words. "You and your companions . . ."; "for they are a wondrous sign." Joshua and Zerubbabel, contemporaries of the prophet Zechariah, were symbols of things to come, prophetic representations of the approaching Kingdom that Jesus[17] would establish in his first appearance.

Zechariah demonstrates just how Joshua and Zerubbabel are to be recognized as a sign of the coming Kingdom of the Messiah, the BRANCH.

> Then he showed me Joshua the high priest standing before the Angel of the LORD. . . . Now Joshua was clothed with filthy garments and was standing before the Angel. Then He answered and spoke to those who stood before Him, saying, "Take away the filthy garments from him." And to him He said, "See, I have removed your iniquity from you, and I will clothe you with rich robes." (Zechariah 3:1, 3–4)

> So he answered and said to me: "This is the word of the LORD to Zerubbabel: Not by might nor by power, but by My Spirit, says the LORD of hosts. Who are you, O great mountain? Before Zerubbabel you shall become a plain! And he shall bring forth the capstone with shouts of Grace, grace to it!" (Zechariah 4:6–7)

---

16. Not to be confused with the Joshua who succeeded Moses and led the Israelites over the Jordan to take possession of the Promised Land.

17. My Servant the BRANCH.

The two witnesses of John's Revelation are the two olive trees of Zechariah's vision. And those two olive trees are signs that represent the cleansing of the New Covenant and the empowering presence of the Spirit in the New Covenant. In other words, they are us, the church, cleansed and empowered, witnesses sent into the world with the hope of the gospel.

TWO OLIVE TREES

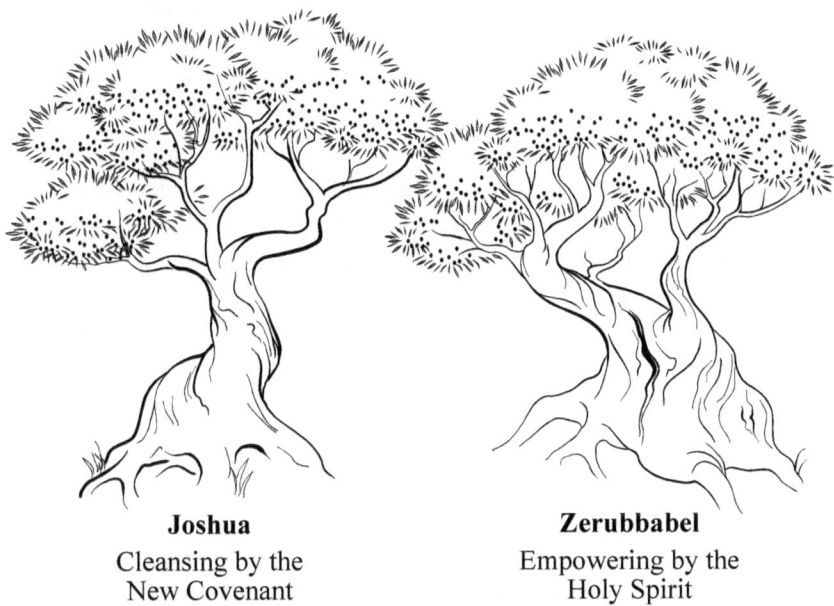

Joshua
Cleansing by the
New Covenant

Zerubbabel
Empowering by the
Holy Spirit

NEW TESTAMENT CHURCH

Come back with me now to our passage in Revelation.

> And I will give power to my two witnesses, and they will prophesy one thousand two hundred and sixty days, clothed in sackcloth. These are the two olive trees and the two lampstands standing before the God of the earth. (Revelation 11:3–4)

The two witnesses of Revelation 11 are the two olive trees of Zechariah—the New Testament church, cleansed, sanctified as priests, and empowered by the Holy Spirit. They are also the two lampstands. With this we are also reminded of Zechariah's prophecy, which had the olive trees either side of a lampstand, but for my mind it is hard to go past how John depicts lampstands in his own writing.

In Revelation 1:20, Christ was seen walking amongst seven lampstands, each of which was one of the seven churches the Revelation was written for. Of those seven, only two were blameless—Smyrna and Philadelphia.

It is obvious who the two witnesses are. They are not a future appearance of Elijah and Moses, or Elijah and Enoch. No, they are the pure, blameless, cleansed, and empowered New Testament church.

Imagine for a moment that you are living at the time of John and that you are a part of the church in Smyrna or Philadelphia. This image of the two witnesses is describing you! What an encouragement to see yourself described in such wondrous language. You will see yourself prophesying in sackcloth and you will completely understand that. In the midst of your suffering and trial, you have a spoken message that you are encouraged to proclaim boldly to the world around you, and you are clothed with an attitude of humble dependance on heaven's empowerment. This passage is about you, the member of the suffering church.

> And if anyone wants to harm them, fire proceeds from their mouth and devours their enemies. And if anyone wants to harm them, he must be killed in this manner. These have power to shut heaven, so that no rain falls in the days of their prophecy; and they have power over waters to turn them to blood, and to strike the earth with all plagues, as often as they desire. (Revelation 11:5-6)

It is so important for us to see ourselves in this striking allusion to the miraculous ministry of the Old Testament prophets Elijah and Moses.[18] As the empowered, cleansed church, we have the enabling and authority of the risen Christ. The two witnesses

---

18. Refer 1 Kings 17:1; James 5:17; Exodus 7:20; 1 Samuel 4:8; Mark 11:23; and John 15:7.

cannot be destroyed, and they preach a word of fire.[19] All this is an encouragement to believers to not fear man, no matter how terrible the persecution you may suffer.[20]

> When they finish their testimony, the beast that ascends out of the bottomless pit will make war against them, overcome them, and kill them. And their dead bodies will lie in the street of the great city which spiritually is called Sodom and Egypt, where also our Lord was crucified. (Revelation 11:7–8)

This is the Revelation's first introduction of the beast, which is detailed more specifically in Revelation 13. It is so prominent in Eschatology that I will presently devote a whole section to it. But for now, it is enough for me to tell you that the beast represents man in opposition to God. As the scene before us unfolds, and as many Christians throughout history have experienced, the beast attacks the witnesses, even bringing about their death.

The great city[21] is not literally Jerusalem, Sodom, or Egypt. It is the earthly city, in opposition to the heavenly city of chapters 21 and 22. It is the camp of the unrighteous, the world as modern Christians call it. Spiritually, it is called Sodom—the city destroyed by God's judgment[22]—and Egypt—also destroyed by God's judgment—where also our Lord was crucified.[23]

> Then those from the peoples, tribes, tongues, and nations will see their dead bodies three-and-a-half days, and not allow their dead bodies to be put into graves. And those who dwell on the earth will rejoice over them, make merry, and send gifts to one another, because these

---

19. Compare with Luke 10:19; Jeremiah 5:14.

20. "And do not fear those who kill the body but cannot kill the soul. But rather fear Him who is able to destroy both soul and body in hell" (Matthew 10:28).

21. The great city also features in Revelation 16:19; 17:18; 18:10, 16, 18–19, 21.

22. Genesis 19:24. Compare also with Isaiah 1:9–10; Ezekiel 16:46, 55.

23. It is noteworthy that Jerusalem is unnamed. John does not want to align the literal city, the City of David, with all its promise and prophetic hope, with Sodom and Egypt.

> two prophets tormented those who dwell on the earth. (Revelation 11:9–10)

Reflect on this, putting yourself in the place of John's original audience, members of the persecuted church of Smyrna or Philadelphia. Throughout the gospel era, there have always been seasons where the church has been violently opposed.[24] For those who live in such times, like John's original audience, it can feel as if the dark forces at work in our world are supreme. But John paints a different picture. The period of death is short-lived.

> Now after the three-and-a-half days the breath of life from God entered them, and they stood on their feet, and great fear fell on those who saw them. And they heard a loud voice from heaven saying to them, "Come up here." And they ascended to heaven in a cloud, and their enemies saw them. (Revelation 11:11–12)

Over the centuries, persecution has often caused the demise of a church in one place or another but, as in verse 11, it always rises. Jesus is our head and he is the resurrection and the life. The gospel simply cannot be chained, and the church cannot be killed. God's Kingdom is an everlasting Kingdom and there is no end to its increase.[25]

> In the same hour there was a great earthquake, and a tenth of the city fell. In the earthquake seven thousand people were killed, and the rest were afraid and gave glory to the God of heaven. (Revelation 11:13)

It is perhaps paradoxical that in times when the church is persecuted the greatest, revival flows in its wake. Despite the worst persecution, the church of Jesus rises and causes even its enemies to give glory to the God of heaven.

---

24. It is probably worth mentioning that even in periods of greatest persecutions, oppression against churches has never been universal. Intense persecution tends to be regional, not systematically spread over entire nations or empires.

25. Isaiah 9:7.

The War of Armageddon

ARMAGEDDON

I find it fascinating that it is not only Christians who are familiar with the name, Armageddon. It features in a lot of popular secular culture. Yet it is found in only one verse of the entire Bible, Revelation 16:16. To understand it, we will look at its context—the pouring out of the sixth bowl of God's wrath.

> Then the sixth angel poured out his bowl on the great river Euphrates, and its water was dried up, so that the way of the kings from the east might be prepared. And I saw three unclean spirits like frogs coming out of the mouth of the dragon, out of the mouth of the beast, and out of the mouth of the false prophet. For they are spirits of demons, performing signs, which go out to the kings of the earth and of the whole world, to gather them to the battle of that great day of God Almighty. "Behold, I am coming as a thief. Blessed is he who watches, and keeps his garments, lest he walk naked and they see his shame." And they gathered them together to the place called in Hebrew, Armageddon. (Revelation 16:12–16)

Before discussing Armageddon in detail, allow me to make a few observations from the passage.

- The scene commences with the Euphrates River drying up to make way for the kings from the east. This is reminiscent of the miraculous overthrow of the ancient city of Babylon in 539BC. At that time, the Medes and Persians, from the east, under King Cyrus, diverted the Euphrates River and marched into the city on the dry riverbed.[26] The passage in Revelation 16 alludes to this as it deals with the overthrow of spiritual Babylon—the world.

- In the visions of the Revelation, John identifies the dragon as Satan.[27] We will show in chapter 6, *When Christ Rules the*

---

26. The scene is also reminiscent of Exodus 14:21; Joshua 3:17; Isaiah 11:16; Jeremiah 51:36; and Zechariah 10:11.

27. Revelation 20:2.

World, that the beast is lost humanity, and the false prophet is false religion and political ideology.

- Note the degeneration of the devil and his hosts across the Biblical narrative. Lucifer was originally a mighty and beautiful angel. By the time of the temptation in the Garden of Eden, he was a serpent. In the New Testament, he is a dragon and his once majestic hosts are nothing but frogs![28]

- The battle of the great day of God Almighty is described in greater detail in chapters 19 and 20 of Revelation, and we will come to that presently, but note: it is not the devil's day, or the beast's day, or the false prophet's day.[29] These three may indeed send out the unclean spirits, but only because it is God's pre-determined plan. It is the great day of God Almighty! He is forever Sovereign!

- With the declaration, "Behold, I am coming as a thief," we are drawn to recognize that this sixth bowl of God's wrath culminates with the Lord's return.[30]

It is in this context, then, that we come to the famous reference to Armageddon, the place where the kings of the earth are gathered together. As John said, the name of the place in Hebrew is *Armageddon*. The Hebrew name—but John wrote in Greek. The problem with that is that not all the Hebrew vocalizations have Greek counterparts. This makes it difficult to transliterate many Hebrew words into Greek. There are two candidates for what John intended: *Ir megiddo*—the city of Megiddo, or *Harmegiddo*—the mountain of Megiddo. Either are acceptable.

---

28. You can see this decaying glory in Ezekiel 28:12b; Genesis 3:1; and Revelation 12:3.

29. A recurring motif throughout the Revelation is that the enemies of God have no power in and of themselves. Time and again you will read expressions like, "It was given to them to do such and such."

30. Compare with 1 Thessalonians 5:2. The Thief in the Night features significantly in prophetic interpretation, so I have devoted a whole section to it in the next chapter.

THE WAR OF ARMAGEDDON

Megiddo is in the plain of Esdraelon and was the site of many Old Testament battles.[31] It is very near to the Valley of Jezreel, another famous ancient battleground.[32] Megiddo and the surrounding region is therefore synonymous, in the Jewish mind of John's time, with battle and divine deliverance. And that is what he is drawing our attention to. It is the place of conflict, the place of retribution.

This fits with the overarching Biblical theme of persecution that the church suffers right up until the return of Christ. At the last, when Christ returns, the enemies of his people are gathered together to the place of final judgment, symbolized by the name *Armageddon*.

GOG AND MAGOG

Perhaps one of the most famous images of Eschatology is the conflict with Gog and Magog, described in detail in Ezekiel 38–39. Because the prophecy centers on the land of Israel, war in the Middle East is widely held to be a precursor to the Second Coming. Nevertheless, as I intimated in chapter 2, *Prophetic Colored Glasses*, Ezekiel's prophecy should not be interpreted literally. Israel is the Old Testament mystery identified in the New Testament church. The Gog/Magog prophecy does not at all envision a Middle Eastern war.

> Thus says the Lord GOD: "Behold, I am against you, O Gog, the chief prince of Meshech and Tubal. I will turn you around, put hooks into your jaws, and lead you out, with all your army, horses, and horsemen, all splendidly clothed, a great company with bucklers and shields, all of them handling swords. Persia, Cush, and Put are with them, all of them with shield and helmet; Gomer and all its troops; the house of Togarmah from the far north and all its troops—many people are with you." (Ezekiel 38:3–6)[33]

---

31. For examples, see 2 Kings 9:27; 2 Kings 23:29–30; and Zechariah 12:11.
32. See 1 Samuel 29:1; 2 Kings 9:14–17; and Hosea 1:4–5.
33. I have taken the liberty of using the Hebrew names for the various people groups. The NKJV understands *Rosh* to be a people group rather than translating it as *chief prince* as most translations.

It is instructive to see these people on a map of the world as Ezekiel would have known it in his time.

The Final Conflict

As you can readily see, Gog's army is drawn from the far north, south, and east—the extremities of Ezekiel's world. The specific nations that are mentioned are not the point of the prophecy. It is where they come from—the ends of the earth. In keeping with the hidden mystery of the church, comprising both Jew and Gentile in the one body, we see a graphic image of persecution against God's people.

The intention of the prophecy is repeated throughout.

> "It will be in the latter days that I will bring you against My land, so that the nations may know Me, when I am

hallowed in you, O Gog, before their eyes." (Ezekiel 38:16)

"Thus I will magnify Myself and sanctify Myself and I will be known in the eyes of many nations. Then they shall know that I am the Lord." (Ezekiel 38:23)

"So I will make My holy name known in the midst of My people Israel, and I will not let them profane My holy name anymore. Then the nations shall know that I am the Lord, the Holy One in Israel." (Ezekiel 39:7)

"I will set My glory among the nations; all the nations shall see My judgment which I have executed, and My hand which I have laid on them. So the house of Israel shall know that I am the Lord their God from that day forward." (Ezekiel 39:21–22)

Of significance, the prophecy culminates in the gift of the Spirit.

"Then they shall know that I am the Lord their God, who sent them into captivity among the nations, but also brought them back to their land, and left none of them captive any longer. And I will not hide My face from them anymore; for I shall have poured out My Spirit on the house of Israel," says the Lord God. (Ezekiel 39:28–29)

So when is this judgment that Ezekiel foresaw? It began most profoundly at the cross. Indeed, it must be so for the context of the prophecy to remain internally consistent. The gift of the Spirit at the close of chapter 39 is clearly a reference to the birth of the church on the day of Pentecost.[34]

The way Eschatology is commonly presented, we are not taught to see judgment commencing at the cross. But it was there, on Golgotha, that the devil, represented by Gog in Ezekiel's prophecy, was overthrown in judgment.[35] Once salvation had been secured

---

34. Consider Acts 2:16–21.
35. See John 16:11; Colossians 2:15; 1 John 3:8; Luke 10:18.

for us by Christ, the promise of the Holy Spirit was poured out on all those who call upon the name of the Lord.[36]

As is typical of New Covenant realities, what began at the cross continues until the return of Christ. In this way, we can see Ezekiel's prophecy unfolding around us even today as God calls people back to himself out of captivity and pours his Spirit on them. At times they will face persecution and feel surrounded by the devil's forces, and indeed this may be true for whole churches and regions, but deliverance is their inheritance. Finally, when Christ returns, the prophecy will come to a close. The devil's end and the judgment of the nations will be complete.

ZECHARIAH'S ACCOUNT OF ARMAGEDDON

Time and again, as we read Old Testament eschatological prophecies, we need to keep our eyes open for God's hidden mystery, the church. Zechariah 12:1—14:21, so often referred to in teachings and commentaries on Ezekiel 38–39, is such a prophecy. It talks of the house of David, the house of Judah, Jerusalem, and Israel. All are images of the New Covenant people of God.

Zechariah's prophecy depicts the present reign of Christ and God's judgment on sin. In many ways, it need not be read with the return of Christ in mind at all. In fact, I think it is better not to look for the return of Christ in its message, as we will shortly see.

The battle depicted in Zechariah 12:2–9 equates very closely with that of chapter 14:1–5 in the second half of the prophecy. I will keep my discussion, for the most part, to this second half and in that way guide you as to how to understand Zechariah's message.

> Behold, the day of the LORD is coming, and your spoil will be divided in your midst. For I will gather all the nations to battle against Jerusalem; the city shall be taken, the houses rifled, and the women ravished. Half of the city shall go into captivity, but the remnant of the people shall not be cut off from the city. (Zechariah 14:1–2)

---

36. Refer Acts 2:1–39.

The War of Armageddon

This describes persecution in general. Unlike the prophecy of Ezekiel 38–39, where fire fell from heaven before the battle, the church in Zechariah's prophecy is overtaken.[37] Persecution is a current reality that believers have faced ever since the time of the apostles. It is not at all surprising then, to find the Old Testament prophets foretelling it. As they peered into the tunnel of time, they saw the realities we would face.

It is probably more in keeping with Zechariah's overall message, however, to acknowledge that persecution began well before the birth of Christ. The story of the Old Testament people of God is a story of almost perpetual conflict with the surrounding nations. It was into that context of suffering and war that Christ came. And so we read in the following verses of Zechariah's prophecy . . .

> Then the LORD will go forth and fight against those nations, as He fights in the day of battle. And in that day His feet will stand on the Mount of Olives, which faces Jerusalem on the east. And the Mount of Olives shall be split in two, from east to west, making a very large valley; half of the mountain shall move toward the north and half of it toward the south. Then you shall flee through My mountain valley, for the mountain valley shall reach to Azal. Yes, you shall flee as you fled from the earthquake in the days of Uzziah king of Judah. Thus the LORD my God will come, and all the saints with You. (Zechariah 14:3–5)

The passage describes Jesus' first appearing, not his second, and has him standing on the Mount of Olives, a poignant setting considering his famous Olivet Discourse that we studied in chapter 3, *Signs of the Times*. In keeping with prophetic symbolism, we are not meant to think that the prophet is foretelling a literal splitting of the Mount of Olives. It is a prophetic declaration of the way of salvation opening to us at Christ's death on the cross.

> It shall come to pass in that day that there will be no light;[38] the lights will diminish. It shall be one day which

---

37. Compare Ezekiel 39:3–5 with Zechariah 14:2.
38. In a sense, this was literally fulfilled at the cross. From that moment of utter darkness, the inextinguishable light of God fell upon our world revealing

> is known to the LORD—neither day nor night. But at evening time it shall happen that it will be light. And in that day it shall be that living waters shall flow from Jerusalem, half of them toward the eastern sea and half of them toward the western sea; in both summer and winter it shall occur. (Zechariah 14:6–8)

What a beautiful passage foretelling the living waters of salvation that Jesus came to release. For those living in the shadow of darkness, sin, and oppression, a place of peace and joy can be found alongside the rivers that flow from his side.[39] Those living waters still flow today for all who call on Jesus' Name.

> All the land shall be turned into a plain from Geba to Rimmon south of Jerusalem. Jerusalem shall be raised up and inhabited in her place from Benjamin's Gate to the place of the First Gate and the Corner Gate, and from the Tower of Hananel to the king's winepresses. The people shall dwell in it; and no longer shall there be utter destruction, but Jerusalem shall be safely inhabited. (Zechariah 14:10–11)

Jerusalem will be elevated, and the mountains flattened. Even in times of persecution, the church is exalted. And those unjust regimes that brutalize God's people are truly the oppressed ones, the flattened, humiliated mountains suffering under the unseen evil hand of powers and principalities in heavenly places.[40]

Zechariah next paints a frightening picture of God's judgment against those who oppress his people. They are like the walking dead—a living, dying hell.

> And this shall be the plague with which the LORD will strike all the people who fought against Jerusalem: their flesh shall dissolve while they stand on their feet, their eyes shall dissolve in their sockets, and their

---

the new way of salvation that has been opened to us.

39. Compare with Joel 3:18; Ezekiel 47:1–12.

40. This is why Jesus told us to pray for our enemies who persecute us. It is they who are in bondage. By praying for them, we acknowledge that even our oppressors are part of our community that we are called to love.

> tongues shall dissolve in their mouths. It shall come to pass in that day that a great panic from the LORD will be among them. Everyone will seize the hand of his neighbor and raise his hand against his neighbor's hand... And it shall come to pass that everyone who is left of all the nations which came against Jerusalem shall go up from year to year to worship the King, the LORD of hosts, and to keep the Feast of Tabernacles. (Zechariah 14:12–13, 16)

The Feast of Tabernacles is the Old Testament festival of thanksgiving for God's protection and guidance into the Promised Land. It is a wonderful image that depicts the celebration of those who turn to Christ for salvation.

> And it shall be that whichever of the families of the earth do not come up to Jerusalem to worship the King, the LORD of hosts, on them there will be no rain. If the family of Egypt will not come up and enter in, they shall have no rain; they shall receive the plague with which the LORD strikes the nations who do not come up to keep the Feast of Tabernacles. This shall be the punishment of Egypt and the punishment of all the nations that do not come up to keep the Feast of Tabernacles. (Zechariah 14:17–19)

Do not get confused by the references to people coming to Jerusalem to keep the Feast of Tabernacles. Many popular teachers of Eschatology believe that the Scriptures foretell the rebuilding of the temple in Jerusalem, and with it, therefore, the reinstatement of the Old Covenant rituals and festivals. We will look at this in detail in chapter 7, *The Mark of the Beast*, and show that this is far from what the Bible says of Christ's return. No, Zechariah's prophecy simply shows the power of the witness of the church in the face of its oppressors. Their joy in the midst of suffering and their overcoming evil with good shows the power of the Kingdom they have inherited in the gospel. The hearts of the world around us are impacted by the light we carry. Despite the opposition that many Christians and churches face around our world, we have great reason to expect nations to be converted as we maintain our confident hope in the gospel.[41]

The verses that follow make this emphatic.

> In that day "HOLINESS TO THE LORD" shall be engraved on the bells of the horses. The pots in the LORD's house shall be like the bowls before the altar. Yes, every pot in Jerusalem and Judah shall be holiness to the LORD of hosts. Everyone who sacrifices shall come and take them and cook in them. In that day there shall no longer be a Canaanite in the house of the LORD of hosts. (Zechariah 14:20–21)

What a compelling image of the power of God's Kingdom coming to bear on the nations of the world. It is not just that God redeems lost and sinful people—he redeems everything in their world. Everything becomes holy, separated for use by the Lord, even kitchen pots. God is not only the God of the temple; he is also God of the kitchen and God of the workplace. When the Kingdom so gets a hold on a people, everything in that community is impacted.

After having seen how to interpret these verses from Zechariah 14, I invite you to look at the entire prophecy[42] in your personal studies. Remember, look for the church veiled in its imagery. But before you do that, I will draw your attention to a verse that is well known in the study of Eschatology.

> And I will pour on the house of David and on the inhabitants of Jerusalem the Spirit of grace and supplication; then they will look on Me whom they pierced. Yes, they will mourn for Him as one mourns for his only sons, and grieve for Him as one grieves for a firstborn. (Zechariah 12:10)

This verse, along with those that follow, speaks prophetically of the salvation of all those who come to Christ, the one we all have pierced.[43] Each of us who believe have looked on Christ's sacrifice

---

41. Compare with 1 Peter 3:15.
42. Zechariah 12:1—14:21.
43. See Isaiah 53:5.

for us and have had that same Spirit of grace and supplication embrace us.

> In that day a fountain shall be opened for the house of David and for the inhabitants of Jerusalem, for sin and for uncleanness. (Zechariah 13:1)

What a wonderful description of the salvation that has come to us through the incredible gift of God!

THE WOMAN IN THE WILDERNESS

As we have now seen, many end times prophecies foretell persecution of the New Testament church. But all is not doom and gloom. God continually declares our victory, a victory that is found in him, not us. Despite the attacks that may assail God's people, and historically these have been many, God protects his Bride and empowers her through the trials she faces.

John's Revelation shows this emphatically through many of its scenes.

> Now a great sign appeared in heaven: a woman clothed with the sun, with the moon under her feet, and on her head a garland of twelve stars. (Revelation 12:1)

With the overt allusion to Joseph's dream in Genesis 37:9–10, the woman's identity is revealed. She is Israel and we will shortly see that John includes under this image the completed people of God, both Old and New Testament people.

> Then being with child, she cried out in labor and in pain to give birth. And another sign appeared in heaven: behold, a great, fiery red dragon having seven heads and ten horns, and seven diadems on his heads. His tail drew a third of the stars of heaven and threw them to the earth. And the dragon stood before the woman who was ready to give birth, to devour her Child as soon as it was born. She bore a male Child who was to rule all nations with a rod of iron. And her Child was caught up to God and His throne. (Revelation 12:2–5)

Such a graphic description of the devil's murderous desire over the Son of God, the child of the woman. This has long been true, even from the very earliest days of our humanity.

> And I will put enmity between you and the woman, and between your seed and her Seed; He shall bruise your head, and you shall bruise His heel. (Genesis 3:15)

Throughout the Old Testament narrative, the dragon constantly sought to kill the children of promise.[44] You will see it in the preponderance of infertility amongst Israel's mothers, the internal battles and murders amongst the people of God themselves, of the warring onslaught of the surrounding nations and their decimation of Israel.

It is in this sense that John means us to understand the dragon drawing a third of the stars of heaven and throwing them to the earth.[45] The stars have already been defined to us in verse one as the people of God. When we read of the dragon throwing a third of the stars to the ground, we are seeing John's description of the devil's assault on God's people. It is not a declaration that a third of the angels followed Satan's leadership.

As we learned earlier in chapter 4, *Uncovering the Apocalypse*, the Revelation is a prophetic answer to the question, Where is God in times of persecution? John's original audience most definitely saw themselves in the image of the stars being swept to the ground. By identifying themselves this way, the prophetic scene is able to abolish their fears when they see the woman taken on the wings of an eagle and nourished in the wilderness.[46]

> Then the woman fled into the wilderness, where she has a place prepared by God, that they should feed her there one thousand two hundred and sixty days. (Revelation 12:6)

Here we see a different portrayal of the wilderness to the normal Biblical picture. The wilderness is often regarded as a place of

---

44. This culminated in the very birth of Christ when Herod killed all the young boys of Bethlehem. See Matthew 2:16.
45. Revelation 12:4.
46. See Revelation 12:14.

testing, a season to endure, where God's people are humbled before being able to step into the fullness of God's promises. And there is a very real truth in that. But this is not the kind of wilderness the woman is taken to. It is a place of protection and provision.[47] In chapter 8, *Prophetic Times*, I will show you how incredibly powerful a message this is for us today when I open up to you Isaiah's vision of eternity.

> And war broke out in heaven: Michael and his angels fought with the dragon; and the dragon and his angels fought, but they did not prevail, nor was a place found for them in heaven any longer. So the great dragon was cast out, that serpent of old, called the Devil and Satan, who deceives the whole world; he was cast to the earth, and his angels were cast out with him. (Revelation 12:7-9)

In this scene a truth is revealed to us that our world desperately needs to learn. The devil is a defeated foe. He once could stand before God and accuse us in the courts of heaven,[48] but he cannot now. Jesus himself said that he saw Satan fall like lightning out of heaven.[49] And it was in the cross that the devil was defeated, stripped of his might and glory.[50]

> Then I heard a loud voice saying in heaven, "Now salvation, and strength, and the kingdom of our God, and the power of His Christ have come, for the accuser of our brethren, who accused them before our God day and night, has been cast down. And they overcame him by the blood of the Lamb and by the word of their testimony, and they did not love their lives to the death." (Revelation 12:10-11)

We have already seen how John uses *testimony* as a powerful repetition throughout the Revelation. The scene in front of us shows us that not only is our testimony in the face of opposition powerful,

---

47. It is most likely an allusion to God sending Elijah into the wilderness to escape the murderous intentions of Queen Jezebel. Refer 1 Kings 17:1-6.
48. See Job 1:6.
49. See Luke 10:18.
50. See Colossians 2:15.

but it is one of the main ways to overcome that very opposition. The key however is the third part of the equation: they did not love their lives to the death. Wherever Christians live in safety and freedom, they do not realize how important it is for us to live as dead people. We have lost our lives for the gospel. Persecuted churches learn the power of this in a way that the rest of us need to be inspired by.

> "Therefore rejoice, O heavens, and you who dwell in them! Woe to the inhabitants of the earth and the sea! For the devil has come down to you, having great wrath, because he knows that he has a short time." Now when the dragon saw that he had been cast to the earth, he persecuted the woman who gave birth to the male Child. But the woman was given two wings of a great eagle, that she might fly into the wilderness to her place, where she is nourished for a time and times and half a time, from the presence of the serpent. (Revelation 12:7–9)

So many teachers of Eschatology paint pictures of horror and doom to come on the world. Armageddon and global conspiracy inspire fear and uncertainty of the future. But John will not allow us to feel overwhelmed during times of turmoil and spiritual unrest. A place has been prepared for us. We are overcomers. Even if members of our family of faith are thrown into prison or executed, we have the blood of the Lamb, the word of our testimony, and we are those who do not cling to this life—we have given ourselves fully to our Savior.

And in this way, we overcome our oppressors. As Tertullian wrote at the close of the second century: "Plures efficimur, quitiens metimur a vobis: semen est sanguis Christianorum"—"The blood of the martyrs is the seed of the Church."[51]

> For behold, the day is coming, burning like an oven, and all the proud, yes, all who do wickedly will be stubble. And the day which is coming shall burn them up," says the LORD of hosts, "that will leave

---

51. *Apologeticus*, L.13. The text is more closely translated: "We multiply when you reap us. The blood of Christians is seed."

them neither root nor branch. But to you who fear My name the Sun of Righteousness shall arise with healing in His wings; and you shall go out and grow fat like stall-fed calves.

MALACHI 4:1–2

6

When Christ Rules the World

> Remember therefore how you have received and heard; hold fast and repent. Therefore if you will not watch, I will come upon you as a thief, and you will not know what hour I will come upon you. (Revelation 3:3)

CHRIST COMING LIKE A thief! What image does that conjure up for you? It is one of the most surprising similes that Jesus used to describe his return.[1] And perhaps one of the least understood, given the vast difference between life in the first and twenty-first centuries. In the ancient world, people heard something very different in the words "thief in the night" than we do today. We think of a cat-burglar, someone who stealthily breaks into buildings. That was not true of a previous world. In the time of Christ, the thief was a marauding plunderer, coming at a time when you would be caught off-guard and unarmed, and so run from your dwelling in fright, leaving it open for ransacking.

---

1. Refer Matthew 24:43: "But know this, that if the husband-master of the house had paid attention to which part of the night, when the guard is on duty, that the thief would come, he would have kept awake and never permitted his house to be broken through." This is my own translation. The Greek has *which watch the thief would come*. I have expanded the expression because in our modern world, we do not typically have watches, i.e. guards on duty keeping the city walls safe at night when everyone is asleep and vulnerable to attack.

But there is a deeper question to be asked. Why did Jesus ever think to liken himself to a thief? It is the antithesis of all he stands for!

THE THIEF IN THE NIGHT

In each passage that describes Jesus coming like a thief, the immediate context invariably shows that what is indicated is the unexpectedness of Christ's return, not the intent to steal things or people away. The analogy of the thief portrays surprise, unexpectedness, and lack of preparation of those Christ comes to upon his return. But it also portrays a frightening aspect to his return. I sometimes wonder that over the centuries, we have presented such a wonderful and beautiful picture of Jesus, that we have overlooked the fearsome side of who he is. Viewed from this perspective, the use of the analogy of a thief in the night makes sense. It is a time not to be trivialized or disregarded.

> It is a fearful thing to fall into the hands of the living God. (Hebrews 10:31)

Paul makes a classic statement concerning the thief in 1 Thessalonians 5.

> But concerning the times and the seasons, brethren, you have no need that I should write to you. For you yourselves know perfectly that the day of the Lord so comes as a thief in the night. For when they say, "Peace and safety!" then sudden destruction comes upon them, as labor pains upon a pregnant woman. And they shall not escape. (1 Thessalonians 5:1–3)

This is a frightening passage. For those who are not under the blood covenant that Christ made available to us in his death on the cross, the day of his return will be a day of destruction. And it will be unexpected! "And they shall not escape!" God does not wink at human sin. He has provided a way of escape, but that way must be entered by humble acceptance of the salvation that Christ bought for us in his death. And not all receive that offer. Christ's coming will be like a thief—a day of fearful and sudden judgment.

> But you, brethren, are not in darkness, so that this Day should overtake you as a thief. You are all sons of light and sons of the day. We are not of the night nor of darkness. Therefore let us not sleep, as others do, but let us watch and be sober. . . For God did not appoint us to wrath, but to obtain salvation through our Lord Jesus Christ. (1 Thessalonians 5:4–6, 9)

Like the rest of humanity, when Christ returns, we too will be surprised[2] but not as by a thief. If you have put your hope in Christ, you are prepared for his return. It is a day of rejoicing and celebration.

> Let the heavens rejoice, and let the earth be glad; let the sea roar, and all its fullness; let the field be joyful, and all that is in it. Then all the trees of the woods will rejoice before the LORD. For He is coming, for He is coming to judge the earth. He shall judge the world with righteousness, and the peoples with His truth. (Psalm 96:11–13)

In 2 Peter 3:10, the coming of the thief is linked to the heavens disappearing with a roar and the earth and everything in it being laid bare!

> But the day of the Lord will come as a thief in the night, in which the heavens will pass away with a great noise, and the elements will melt with fervent heat; both the earth and the works that are in it will be burned up. (2 Peter 3:10)

Christ's coming ushers in the final judgment of the world and introduces the new heavens and earth. That is a confronting assertion because it is a widespread belief that final judgment occurs a

---

2. It would be a strange person who would not raise an eyebrow at the shout of exaltation of heaven's angels, of the voice of the chief angel, of the great trumpet call, and of the visible return of Christ in the air! See 1 Thessalonians 4:16–17.

thousand years after Christ returns, not commensurate with it. So let us look at this in detail.

THE MILLENNIUM

In Revelation 20, we read of a thousand year reign of Christ (the millennium), of the devil chained in the Abyss, of two resurrections, and of a massive conflict followed by a great day of judgment. The prophecy is fascinating and demands attention in a book like this.

Interestingly, this is the only passage in the whole Bible that explicitly talks of a thousand year time period. We have already discussed the Revelation in broad strokes. Let me now guide you through its description of the millennium and show how John intended us to interpret it.

> Then I saw an angel coming down from heaven, having the key to the bottomless pit and a great chain in his hand. He laid hold of the dragon, that serpent of old, who is the Devil and Satan, and bound him for a thousand years; and he cast him into the bottomless pit, and shut him up, and set a seal on him, so that he should deceive the nations no more till the thousand years were finished. But after these things he must be released for a little while. (Revelations 20:1–3)

John saw an angel seize the dragon, binding him for a thousand years. So many people think this has not happened yet. But the New Testament clearly declares Satan's bondage as a present reality.[3] It is essential that believers—born-again sons and daughters of God, called by his matchless Name—are aware that right now we are seated with Christ in heavenly places. When a teaching declares that the devil was not bound at the cross, it leads God's people into a fearful warfare they need rescue from. Rather, we are to understand that though we wrestle against powers and principalities, we are enforcing a victory that is already ours in Christ.

---

3. See Luke 10:18–19; Luke 11:20–22; Colossians 2:15.

For we do not wrestle against flesh and blood, but against principalities, against powers, against the rulers of the darkness of this age, against spiritual hosts of wickedness in the heavenly places. Therefore take up the whole armor of God, that you may be able to withstand in the evil day, and having done all, to stand. (Ephesians 6:12–13)

Contrary to how spiritual warfare and the armor of God is often taught, the way we wrestle is to clothe ourselves in Jesus' righteousness, shield ourselves with faith and the Word of God, and stand! It is a fight that looks like standing. The lie of the enemy is to get us away from this simple truth and to rely on our own efforts.

As John shows us in Revelation 20, we do not fight a free agent. We fight one who is powerless before Christ's might. Satan's biggest weapon is the lie that comes from his mouth; that he is powerful, that he is not bound, that he can conquer us. This lie can only hold sway over us if we give place to it.

Sadly, many teachings about the millennium feed into this error, and Christians the world over expect this life to be marked by struggle and war, not victory. It could not be further from the truth. Victory over the devil was one of Jesus' chief objectives on earth and he gloriously achieved it at the cross.[4] The Kingdom of God has already, and decisively, intercepted the history of man.[5] Despite the devil's activity in our world, and the very real suffering which he inflicts on humanity, it is imperative that we see that he is a bound and defeated foe. The Kingdom must prevail. We will never see nations bow en masse to Christ if we believe otherwise.

How can it be, then, that the devil is bound for only a thousand years? Jesus' death and resurrection were twice that long ago. This is where John's writing is so misunderstood. The thousand years simply depicts a long time. John used an idiom that was a familiar part of his first century Jewish language.[6] The binding of the devil

---

4. John 19:30; 1 John 3:8b.

5. Refer to Matthew 12:28; Luke 17:20–21; and Colossians 1:13.

6. For Biblical examples, consider Psalm 50:10; Psalm 84:10; Job 9:3. In each case, it is abundantly clear that we are not meant to understand the literal use of the number, one thousand. (As if God only owns the cattle on a thousand hills and not all the cattle of all the hills. Or that one day in the courts of

during this period simply refers to his limited power throughout the Christian age, a power that was overcome at the cross.

In the passage we are studying, John portrayed the devil as being kept from deceiving the nations. Let us explore that thought further. We know that the devil is the spirit that actively energizes the non-Christian world.[7] If God's people are the devil's primary human targets, and we know that we are, why has he not united the disbelieving world together to stamp out all trace of Christianity? He attempted that very thing in the ancient world, before Christ, particularly in the Egyptian, Assyrian, Babylonian, Greek, and early Roman Empires. Yet he has not done it at all in this gospel era. He has been successful on occasion in uniting the government of an occasional nation against the church, but we have not seen a global Empire since Rome. Why not? He empowers all non-believers, why has he not caused them to come together against God's people? He did it before Christ, why not after?

In answer to that important question, John says the devil is bound so that he should deceive the nations no more. I want to underline the plural word, *nations*. Though he is actively at work in the disobedient, he has no power to unite the world in opposition to Christ and his church. He has been thrown into the Abyss, kept from deceiving the nations as a whole.[8]

Having declared the devil's bondage, John next described the victorious church.

> And I saw thrones, and they sat on them, and judgment was committed to them. Then I saw the souls of those who had been beheaded for their witness to Jesus and for the word of God, who had not worshiped the beast or his image, and had not received his mark on their foreheads or on their hands. And they lived and reigned with Christ for a thousand years. But the rest of the dead did not live again until the thousand years were finished.

---

the Lord is not as good as one thousand and one days elsewhere.)

7. Ephesians 2:2.

8. This conclusion finds confirmation in verses 7–9 of our text. The first thing the devil does when he is released from his prison is to incite rebellion in the hearts of the entire unbelieving world. But we will come to that presently.

> This is the first resurrection. Blessed and holy is he who has part in the first resurrection. Over such the second death has no power, but they shall be priests of God and of Christ, and shall reign with Him a thousand years. (Revelation 20:4–6)

Who are those on the thrones to whom judgment is given? It is us, believers, the children of the Kingdom. Because most of us have been taught to see this passage in terms of the return of Christ, when we see the word judgment, we think of the final judgment. And we miss an important aspect of the Christian life. Part of what Jesus has won for us at the cross is to establish a Kingdom in which his blood-bought family have authority. Right now, we have authority to judge in matters pertaining to this life.[9] We are sealed by God's Holy Spirit and do not have the beast's mark.[10] It is essential for believers to understand that we reign with Christ. Right now![11]

"They came to life." How can it be said that we have already taken part in the first resurrection? Surely, the passage talks about those who are resurrected at Christ's return? The widespread belief across our contemporary Christian world is that there are two literal resurrections. The first is the resurrection of believers when Christ returns. The second is the final resurrection, after the millennium when the rest of the dead rise immediately prior to the Great White Throne—Judgment Day. Appeal is made to our passage in Revelation 20, which clearly describes the two resurrection events.

Hold on to your seats, because what I am about to show you is likely to challenge most of what you have ever learned about the resurrection.

Did you know that this is the only passage in the Bible that even suggests two distinct and separate resurrections at the end?[12] That in itself may not mean much to you, but because teachers and preachers believe there will be two separate resurrections associated

---

9. Compare with 1 Corinthians 6:2–3.
10. This thought will be expanded in chapter 7, *The Mark of the Beast*.
11. See Romans 5:17; 1 Peter 2:9; and Revelation 1:6.
12. Caution always needs to be made in developing a doctrine that rests on one Scripture alone.

with Jesus' return, they are predisposed to miss the many Scriptures that explicitly declare that there will be only one resurrection, and that it will occur at the very end of the age.[13] We need to let the plain teaching of the New Testament be our guide to the Revelation, not the other way round.

At this point, you are probably confused. What does John mean if he is not talking about two resurrections at Christ's return? It is simple, really. Elsewhere in the New Testament, the Scripture does speak of resurrection in a symbolic way. It is the rebirth.[14]

When John declares that those who have taken part in the first resurrection are blessed and holy, he is speaking of all believers. Right now, you are blessed. Right now, you are holy. Right now, you have crossed from death to life. You are alive in Christ. The church is victorious in this world! Hell's gates cannot stand before the mighty church of God.[15] We are now in the glorious millennium! There are two ages that God in his Word has told us to concern ourselves with, this present age and the age to come.[16]

At the end of this present era, the *thousand years* as John calls it, immediately upon the general resurrection of the dead, the devil will inflame the hearts of all the ungodly.

> Now when the thousand years have expired, Satan will be released from his prison and will go out to deceive the nations which are in the four corners of the earth, Gog and Magog, to gather them together to battle, whose number is as the sand of the sea. They went up on the breadth of the earth and surrounded the camp of the saints and the beloved city. And fire came down from God out of heaven and devoured them. The devil, who

---

13. Refer Daniel 12:2; Acts 24:15; Matthew 13:24–30.

14. "Therefore we were buried with Him through baptism into death, that just as Christ was raised from the dead by the glory of the Father, even so we also should walk in newness of life." See also Colossians 2:12–13 ". . . buried with Him in baptism, in which you also were raised with Him through faith in the working of God, who raised Him from the dead. And you, being dead in your trespasses and the uncircumcision of your flesh, He has made alive together with Him." (Romans 6:4).

15. See Matthew 16:18; Luke 10:19; and James 4:7.

16. Compare with Matthew 12:32; Mark 10:30; and Ephesians 1:21.

deceived them, was cast into the lake of fire and brimstone where the beast and the false prophet are. And they will be tormented day and night forever and ever. (Revelation 20:7–10)

The rage the devil inspires will be directed towards the church.[17] Yet you will notice that before a hand is laid on anyone, the fire of judgment engulfs the devil and ungodly mankind.[18] And that is the message that popular Christianity has not understood. The day of Christ's return is the day that Christ judges the world! As C.S. Lewis wrote, "When the author walks on to the stage, the play is over."[19]

How does this way of reading Revelation 20 fit with the rest of the New Testament?

In 2 Thessalonians 1, Paul explains that upon Christ's return, all those who do not know God will be punished with everlasting destruction and exclusion from the presence of his majesty. And it happens when Jesus comes back.

> . . . and to give you who are troubled rest with us when the Lord Jesus is revealed from heaven with His mighty angels, in flaming fire taking vengeance on those who do not know God, and on those who do not obey the gospel of our Lord Jesus Christ. These shall be punished with everlasting destruction from the presence of the Lord and from the glory of His power, when He comes, in that Day, to be glorified in His saints and to be admired among all those who believe. (2 Thessalonians 1:7–10)

The Apostle Peter paints the same picture.

> But the day of the Lord will come as a thief in the night, in which the heavens will pass away with a great noise,

---

17. Verses 7–9 identify the church by the expressions, *the camp of the saints* and *the beloved city*. The passage compares with Ezekiel 38–39.

18. Compare with Ezekiel 38:22. It is obvious that John is directing us back to Ezekiel 38–39 by his parenthetical use of the expression *Gog and Magog*. Refer to our discussion in the last chapter.

19. C.S. Lewis, *Mere Christianity* (New York: Simon and Schuster Touchstone, 1996), p65.

and the elements will melt with fervent heat; both the earth and the works that are in it will be burned up. (2 Peter 3:10)

In his first letter to the Corinthians, Paul declares emphatically that there will be one, and only one, final resurrection and that it will immediately precede the judgment.[20] His concern in writing to the Corinthians is that they understand the implications of the resurrection for Christians. Because of this, many teachers align it with their understanding of the Revelation's first resurrection. The passage clearly reveals, however, Paul's doctrine of the resurrection in general. Let us look at it.

- When Jesus returns, the dead in Christ are resurrected.

    But each one in his own order: Christ the firstfruits, afterward those who are Christ's at His coming. (1 Corinthians 15:23)

- Jesus reigns until all his enemies under his feet and only then does he deliver the kingdom to God the Father.

    Then comes the end, when He delivers the kingdom to God the Father, when He puts an end to all rule and all authority and power. For He must reign till He has put all enemies under His feet. (1 Corinthians 15:24–25)

- The last of Christ's enemies is death.

    The last enemy that will be destroyed is death. (1 Corinthians 15:26)

Did you follow the progression of Paul's argument? Christ reigns until all his enemies are placed under his feet. The last of these enemies is death. At that point, the resurrection occurs. And understandably so. If death has finally been removed, it necessarily

---

20. Paul's full enunciation of the resurrection of the dead is found in 1 Corinthians 15:23–54.

means that the dead are raised. The end comes after Christ has destroyed all dominion and power, the last of which is death.

Christ's reign is now! And to be honest, that should be obvious to us. When he returns, the last enemy, death, is swallowed up in victory. The manifestation of this is the resurrection of the dead. In the meantime, successive enemies of the cross, those things that Christ died to redeem us from, are put under his feet. Get that revelation in your heart and it will change everything for you. We do not wait for Christ to come back before the world around us can be changed for the good. We have the authority that comes with our identity as his blood-bought children and we have the power that comes with the presence of his world-transforming Holy Spirit.

Some will question, though, that Paul did not refer to non-Christians, only believers rising from the dead in 1 Corinthians 15. But of course, he never was going to talk about non-believers in the context of 1 Corinthians 15. It was irrelevant to his purpose. The whole point of his writing was to explain to the Christians of Corinth what would happen to them when Christ returns. But it is easy to discern his teaching regarding the resurrection in general. His logic is easy to extrapolate beyond his immediate discussion. Death is the last enemy that will be placed under Christ's feet. This is nothing short of the resurrection of all who have died.

JUDGMENT DAY

> Then I saw a great white throne and Him who sat on it, from whose face the earth and the heaven fled away. And there was found no place for them. And I saw the dead, small and great, standing before God, and books were opened. And another book was opened, which is the Book of Life. And the dead were judged according to their works, by the things which were written in the books. The sea gave up the dead who were in it, and Death and Hades delivered up the dead who were in them. And they were judged, each one according to his works. Then Death and Hades were cast into the lake of fire. This is the second death. And anyone not found

written in the Book of Life was cast into the lake of fire.
(Revelation 20:11–15)

The earth and the heaven fled away.[21] I do not want you to think however, that this means the planet suffers some sort of cataclysmic destruction. We have already learned that, upon Christ's return, we are clothed with immortality. The same thing happens with our entire world and universe. Way back in the beginning, when man fell in the garden, the whole cosmos was subjected to corruption. When Jesus returns, everything will finally be restored, the corrupt clothed with incorruption.[22] Our passage in Revelation 20 commences with the earth and sky fleeing. This merely sets the scene for this rebirth of the created order.[23]

At the judgment, all stand before the Lord.[24] The dead are judged according to what they had done as recorded in the books.[25] Death is destroyed convincingly at this time, showing the full power of the Life that Jesus won for us at the cross.[26] Whoever's name was not found written in the Book of Life[27] was cast into the lake of fire—the second death.

This is sobering. Judgment is final. And based upon people's works. Even Christians face this judgment.[28] Obviously, we are not to think we are saved by our works. That would undermine the cross and all that Jesus did for us. We are saved by grace, not our

---

21. Compare also with Psalm 102:25–27; Isaiah 51:6; Mark 13:31; and 2 Peter 3:10.

22. Compare with Romans 8:19–21.

23. Compare with Revelation 21:1.

24. See also Romans 14:10; 2 Corinthians 5:10.

25. The idea of God keeping books in relation to people's actions is a common Old Testament theme. See for example Daniel 7:10; Psalm 56:8; Psalm 139:16; and Malachi 3:16. The thought does not demand the literal making of books in heaven to record our actions. It merely shows that nothing goes without God's attention.

26. Compare with 1 Corinthians 15:26.

27. For references relating to the Book of Life, see Exodus 32:32; Psalm 69:28; Philippians 4:3; Revelation 3:5; and Revelation 13:8.

28. See Matthew 12:37; Matthew 16:27; Romans 2:6–10; Romans 14:10–12; 1 Corinthians 3:13; and 2 Corinthians 5:10.

works. Yet, at the judgment, it is our works that reveal whether we have received the gracious pardon of God through Christ or not. Works are important![29]

All this points to one thing: When Christ returns, he will judge the world. We should not hang on to a vain hope that there will be a period of respite in which people are able to repent. I assume that you who read this book are a believer, but if you have not trusted in Christ as your Savior, if you have not come back to him and believed on the One that died for you, do not presume on his kindness. Today is the day of salvation. Do not pin your hopes on coming to him when it is all over.

If anyone would be sure of salvation they must find peace with God today, not tomorrow, because tomorrow may see our awesome Judge sitting in judgment against the devil and all those who do not know God and do not obey his gospel.[30] The Lord is at hand!

A THOUSAND YEARS IS LIKE A DAY

> Knowing this first: that scoffers will come in the last days, walking according to their own lusts, and saying, "Where is the promise of His coming? For since the fathers fell asleep, all things continue as they were from the beginning of creation." (2 Peter 3:3–4)

This is an important passage for today. We have had so much teaching that has boldly declared that the Lord was about to return in the near future that it would be easy to scoff at any mention of him coming back. To the question "Where is this coming he promised?" Peter replies that God does not consider time in the same manner as us. For him, a day is like a thousand years and a thousand years are like a day.

---

29. Where there is no evidence of a repentant lifestyle, a person should not presume that they have found peace with God through Christ. See John 5:24–29; Galatians 6:7–8; and James 2:14–19.

30. 2 Thessalonians 1:7–10.

When Christ Rules the World

> But, beloved, do not forget this one thing, that with the Lord one day is as a thousand years, and a thousand years as one day. The Lord is not slack concerning His promise, as some count slackness, but is longsuffering toward us, not willing that any should perish but that all should come to repentance. (2 Peter 3:8–9)

This does not mean that God is in a dimension outside of time or that he calls one thousand year periods, days. What Peter is saying is that the length of time between the cross and the return of Christ does not reveal a tardy God, but rather, a merciful God. When that day does finally come, however, it will be revealed in awesome power and judgment.

> But the day of the Lord will come as a thief in the night, in which the heavens will pass away with a great noise, and the elements will melt with fervent heat; both the earth and the works that are in it will be burned up. Therefore, since all these things will be dissolved, what manner of persons ought you to be in holy conduct and godliness, looking for and hastening the coming of the day of God, because of which the heavens will be dissolved, being on fire, and the elements will melt with fervent heat? Nevertheless we, according to His promise, look for new heavens and a new earth in which righteousness dwells. (2 Peter 3:10–13)

At Jesus' return, not only will the wicked be laid bare, but the heavens themselves will pass away. The elements melting in fervent heat is not a prophetic reference to the splitting of the atom or to nuclear holocaust, as I have heard preached. The elements of the ancients were not the chemical elements of the Periodic Table as we understand the term today, but simply earth, wind, water, and fire. What Peter is saying is that everything that is corrupt or subject to decay will be made new. The earth passing away introduces Peter's major tenet that God recreates the heavens and earth. This recreation of the cosmos is the natural world's corollary to our own recreation as sons of God.[31]

---

31. See Romans 8:20–21.

Everything melts in Jesus' presence. That which has been subject to corruption cannot remain when everything has finally been placed under his feet. It is at once a time of rejoicing and fear. Rejoicing, in that judgment has come at last, injustice and curse consumed by the fire of his holy proximity. Fear, in that we will stand before the Holy One, the Majestic One, the Creator of the heavens and the earth, and give an account.

> Therefore, beloved, looking forward to these things, be diligent to be found by Him in peace, without spot and blameless; and consider that the longsuffering of our Lord is salvation.
>
> 2 Peter 3:14–15

7

The Mark of the Beast

ANTICHRIST, THE BEAST, 666. These are themes that fuel wild speculation in today's popular belief systems. Throughout the centuries, Antichrist has been identified multiple times. That should leave us dumbfounded—firstly in the absurdity of the conjectured candidates and secondly in that people believed them! I mean, as if God had spoken specifically about Kissinger, Hitler, or Sadam Hussein![1]

Whenever I have been invited to talk about these topics, I have been amazed how fearful many believers are about the future. Questionable teachings about the state of the world prior to Christ's return do not help. We find ourselves retreating from a world that we are supposed to bring hope to. And we fail to step into the fulness of the inheritance that is ours in Christ. Because of wrong teaching, many Christians fear international policy negotiations and government innovations. Maybe of more concern is that these same teachings have taught Christians to live in suspicion of all who disagree with their views—it certainly is not the fruit of faith

---

1. I once spoke at a Pentecostal Denominational Conference in Australia, and proved from the Scripture that the denomination's National Chairman was the devil, the Vice-Chairman was Antichrist, and the National Secretary was the False Prophet! It was a joke of course, and well received, but it did serve to illustrate that you can make all sorts of wild conclusions if you misuse the Biblical texts.

and love that you would expect from the proclamation of the hope of the Second Coming!

So what are we to make of it all? To begin unravelling what the Bible says about Antichrist, the beast, and 666, we need to look at some key texts from John's Revelation.

THE BEAST OUT OF THE SEA

Revelation 13 begins with a vision of a beast rising from the sea.[2] A second beast then rises from the earth and institutes mandatory worship of the first beast among all who dwell on the earth.[3] This is achieved by placing a mark on the right hand or forehead of every person who worships the beast and denying access to commerce and trade to those who refuse the mark. The mark they receive is the beast's name, or the number of his name, 666. Let us begin by looking at this mark in detail.

> He causes all, both small and great, rich and poor, free and slave, to receive a mark on their right hand or on their foreheads, and that no one may buy or sell except one who has the mark or the name of the beast, or the number of his name. Here is wisdom. Let him who has understanding calculate the number of the beast, for it is the number of a man: His number is 666. (Revelation 13:16–18)

The text is regularly cited with regard to the identity of the Antichrist and of a supposed global cashless society.[4] It is the only passage in the whole Bible, however, where we have any reference at all to the mark of the beast. Reader beware. So how are we to understand it?

---

2. Revelation 13:1–10.

3. Revelation 13:11–18.

4. The belief in a future cashless society is relatively new, and is popularly held amongst Dispensationalists.

THE MARK OF THE BEAST, 666

> Here is wisdom. Let him who has understanding calculate the number of the beast, for it is the number of a man: His number is 666. (Revelation 13:18)

John did not say, "This calls for knowledge. If anyone has access to the correct facts, let him calculate the beast's number." It does not depend on having access to the right information but on being a person with understanding. It is a call for wisdom![5] Anyone, even if they lived in the second century, could calculate the beast's number. All they need is wisdom. Whatever John meant, then, it cannot be anything to do with a bankcard, computer code, laser tattoo, or implanted chip technology. These would require access to the right information, not wisdom.

John poses a riddle for us—to calculate the number of the beast—but we hit a snag when reading it in English. You will recall a previous discussion we had concerning the use of the definite article in the Greek language of the New Testament. Let me complicate it one step further. There is no indefinite article, *a*, in New Testament Greek. That means that when no article precedes a noun in a Greek sentence, it could be because it is indefinite, but as we have seen previously, it could be that the Greek author simply did not feel to use the definite article. Where no article exists before a noun in the Greek New Testament, the translator must determine

---

5. It is worth noting that the Biblical peoples used language, in general, differently than we do in English. Our modern worldview is very much geared towards the mind, reason, rationality. The culture of the Biblical peoples was geared towards heart matters, relationship. Worldview informs language. For example: Adam knew his wife and she conceived—Genesis 4:1. In English, knowledge is cognitive. In Hebrew, it is relational. Adam was intimate with Eve. He knew her. Another example: God remembered Noah—Genesis 8:1. It is a relational remembrance. God took his relationship with Noah into consideration. It is not as if God had forgotten about Noah cognitively and fortunately his memory was jogged. In the verse we are looking at in Revelation, wisdom is a heart wisdom. John is calling for those who are pure in heart. "But the wisdom that is from above is first pure, then peaceable, gentle, willing to yield, full of mercy and good fruits, without partiality and without hypocrisy." (James 3:17).

whether to use *the* or *a*. The context nearly always directs the translator's choice.

In the verse we are considering, the NIV translation has a footnote that reads, "Or *is humanity's number*." By that, the NIV translators are drawing attention to the lack of the article. In English, we can say, "It is man's number," meaning mankind's number, or we can say, "It is a man's number," meaning the number of a specific, though unidentified, man. New Testament Greek cannot make this distinction, so it is left to the context to determine which way the sentence should be translated. And therein lies the problem associated with Revelation 13:18.

I have quoted Revelation 13:18 above from the NKJV. Its translators believe that John was talking about a specific person. This fits their beliefs about the return of Christ. So they translate: *it is the number of a man*. It is surprisingly easy to show, however, that John was not referring to an individual man but to mankind in general.

We typically read Revelation 13:18 as John giving us clues to solve his riddle. But this is far from the case. John gave us the answer to the riddle! I find it difficult to fathom how so many teachers miss this. Let me put the verse in my own vernacular to show you how easily it reads.

"This calls for wisdom. If anyone has insight and is without guile, let him calculate the number of the beast. What number would best represent the beast? What answer do you give? You should give man's number, because that is who the beast is—man. Man's number is 666. Man—forever trying to act as God and forever failing, forever aiming at God's perfection, seven, and forever falling short. Always six, never seven; always found wanting—666."

There is no mystery in 666. It is a symbolic number that represents fallen man in his unsuccessful attempt to exalt himself to the status of God. The very verse that confuses so many gives not only the number of the beast, but also his identity, i.e. mankind without Christ. This is a much more satisfying interpretation of this solitary reference to 666 and closely fits the Biblical narrative. But it is so much more challenging an interpretation—without Christ, every human social structure is ultimately pitted against him! Every human social structure!

HOW DOES THIS COMPARE TO THE BEAST'S DESCRIPTION IN THE REVELATION?

The beast from the sea is described in detail in chapters 13:1–10 and 17:6–17.

> Then I stood on the sand of the sea. And I saw a beast rising up out of the sea, having seven heads and ten horns, and on his horns ten crowns, and on his heads a blasphemous name. Now the beast which I saw was like a leopard, his feet were like the feet of a bear, and his mouth like the mouth of a lion. The dragon gave him his power, his throne, and great authority. And I saw one of his heads as if it had been mortally wounded, and his deadly wound was healed. And all the world marveled and followed the beast. (Revelation 13:1–3)

We see an obvious allusion to the four beasts of Daniel's vision in the Old Testament.[6] Those beasts represented four world empires—Babylonian, Persian, Greek, and Roman.[7] Because John's beast contains aspects of all of Daniel's beasts, he is not intending to describe a unique, end time world government, but is depicting all government. The beast represents man, governing himself apart from, and ultimately in opposition to, Christ.[8]

---

6. Refer Daniel 7:3–7. John's beast carries the likeness of all of Daniel's beasts. Its ten horns compare with Daniel 7:7b. Its resemblance to a leopard compares with Daniel 7:6. The feet of a bear compares with Daniel 7:5. The mouth of a lion compares with Daniel 7:4.

7. This is universally accepted amongst Bible commentators and is acknowledged in all schools of Eschatology.

8. An interesting aside is found in the order in which John alludes to Daniel's beasts. Daniel looked forward in time and saw the Babylonian (lion), Persian (bear), Greek (leopard), and Roman (ten horned beast) Empires. John looked back on those same empires, so, when describing the beast from the sea, placed them in the reverse order—Roman (ten horned beast), Greek (leopard), Persian (bear), and Babylonian (lion).

The beast had a fatal wound that had been healed to the astonishment of the world. The literal translation reads *as having been slain*. It is the same expression John used to describe the Lamb in Revelation 5:6.

> And I saw, and look!, in the midst of the throne and of the four living ones, and in the midst of the elders, a Lamb stood as having been slain, having seven horns and seven eyes, which are the seven spirits of God that have been sent[9] into all the land. (Revelation 5:6, my own literal translation)

> And I saw one of its heads as having been slain to death and its death wound was healed and the whole land wondered in admiration after the beast.[10] (Revelation 13:3, my own literal translation)

John clearly intends us to see the implications of his choice of words. The Lamb as though slain is worshiped by all in heaven. The beast, with its head as though slain, is marveled by all on the earth. Whether man's political and ideological systems are oppressive or not, John's description of the beast shows it to be the antithesis of Christ, the Lamb who stands in the midst of the throne. It is the manifestation of the driving force behind man's attempted self-determination.

Whenever a corrupt system is overturned or an oppressive dictator is unseated and the beast's head appears to have been killed, even if it may be replaced by good, democratic governance and humanitarian ideology, the spirit behind it remains unchanged, an impotent reflection of the resurrection of Christ. As a collective whole, we are always drawn to marvel at our ideological victories, and we always have a political response to our defeats. However, any system outside the direct Lordship of Christ is, in the end, simply another iteration of the beast.

This is enough to establish the proposition that the beast is man in self-governance, but perhaps it is important to show you

---

9. With a commission. The word is the one we get our word *apostle* from.
10. The word denotes a wild, dangerous animal.

THE MARK OF THE BEAST

how to understand more fully the appearance of the beast's form. To do this, we will look at John's description in Revelation 17.

> So he carried me away in the Spirit into the wilderness. And I saw a woman sitting on a scarlet beast which was full of names of blasphemy, having seven heads and ten horns... The beast that you saw was, and is not, and will ascend out of the bottomless pit and go to perdition. And those who dwell on the earth will marvel, whose names are not written in the Book of Life from the foundation of the world, when they see the beast that was, and is not, and yet is. Here is the mind which has wisdom: The seven heads are seven mountains on which the woman sits. There are also seven kings. Five have fallen, one is, and the other has not yet come. And when he comes, he must continue a short time. (Revelation 17:3, 8–10)

John once again calls for wisdom, not knowledge. A wise Christian from John's time could be expected to understand. Conversely, a foolish one never would, no matter how much he knew!

The seven heads are seven hills. This does not specifically refer to the city of Rome, built on its seven hills. That would render the call for wisdom meaningless.[11] In Hebrew literature, hills and mountains refer to seats of power or kingdoms.[12] John states that the heads are also seven kings. This refers again to seven kingdoms. Five had fallen, one was then in existence at the time of John, the other had not yet come. Keep in mind, the Revelation is built on symbolism. The number of kingdoms is likewise symbolic. Five had fallen, therefore John was living in the sixth. The climax, the seventh, was about to happen. Specific kingdoms are not intended to be identified.

> The ten horns which you saw are ten kings who have received no kingdom as yet, but they receive authority for one hour as kings with the beast. These are of one mind, and they will give their power and authority to the

---

11. I am sure, nevertheless, that John's original audience saw a reference to Rome in this image. But it is a bigger allusion than merely to the Roman Empire of John's day.

12. For examples, see Jeremiah 51:25 and Ezekiel 35:2.

> beast. These will make war with the Lamb, and the Lamb will overcome them, for He is Lord of lords and King of kings; and those who are with Him are called, chosen, and faithful. (Revelation 17:12–14)

The ten horns are ten kings who have no kingdom, but who receive authority with the beast for one hour. In that they have no kingdom, they are not kings in any true sense and their perceived reign is only for a short time. As we have already seen, John's description of the beast is meant to draw us back to Daniel's prophecies, and these ten allude to the ten horns of Daniel's fourth beast, and also bring to mind the ten toes of Nebuchadnezzar's dream statue.[13] Daniels four beasts have long been shown to have fulfilment in the ancient world—we are not meant to look for fulfilment in a future world government. Overlaying the allusion to Daniel's prophecy, John uses the number ten in an idiomatically Hebrew way, the number that depicts completion. The ten horns represent the fulness of all would-be kings and would-be leaders, deriving their authority from within their own humanity. And destined to fall.

This is by far a better understanding of the ten horns. So many prophetic interpretations try to align them with specific end time world leaders. But they miss the emphatic teaching of Jesus and the New Testament as a whole. No one knows when Christ will return. Any interpretation that concludes, for whatever reason, that Christ cannot appear in the next half hour fails to acknowledge the imminence of Christ's return.[14]

We conclude once again that it is man who is depicted by the first beast, always drawn irresistibly to worship himself and his Christless systems and philosophies.

> And all the world marveled and followed the beast. So they worshiped the dragon who gave authority to the beast; and they worshiped the beast, saying, "Who is like the beast? Who is able to make war with him?" (Revelation 13:3b–4)

---

13. See Daniel 7:7 and Daniel 2:42.

14. Consider Matthew 24:42, 44; Luke 12:40; Philippians 4:5; 1 Thessalonians 5:2; James 5:9; 1 John 2:18.

The Mark of the Beast

They worshiped the dragon. Without even realizing it, in worshipping himself, man pays homage to the power that works within. This is such a graphic image of the tragic state of lost humanity. Not only are we far from our loving Creator, but we actively worship the enemy of all that is good, the devil.

> And he was given a mouth speaking great things and blasphemies, and he was given authority to continue for forty-two months. (Revelation 13:5)

The beast speaks arrogant and blasphemous words against God,[15] so typical of the spirit within. Yet his time is limited—forty-two months.[16] For all his boasting, he can only exercise authority for the time set by God.

> It was granted to him to make war with the saints and to overcome them. And authority was given him over every tribe, tongue, and nation. All who dwell on the earth will worship him, whose names have not been written in the Book of Life of the Lamb slain from the foundation of the world. (Revelation 13:7–8)

Perhaps shockingly, we see here that as is the nature of the devil, so is the nature of man. The devil is opposed to God and therefore to God's people. In like manner, man in his self-determining independence, makes war with God by persecuting his people and is thereby revealed as being the weapon of oppression in the devil's hand.[17] The completeness of the devil's influence over mankind is shown in verse 8. In failing to worship the one true God, our world worships gods of its own making. Effectively, we worship ourselves, the creators of our gods. Only the redeemed, the people of God, those with the seal of the Holy Spirit, written in the Lamb's Book of Life, are free from the devil's tyranny.

---

15. Compare also with Daniel 7:25.

16. I will discuss the reference to forty-two months in chapter 8, *Prophetic Times*.

17. Compare also with Revelation 12:17.

THE LOST MESSAGE OF THE END TIMES

THE BEAST OUT OF THE EARTH

> Then I saw another beast coming up out of the earth, and he had two horns like a lamb and spoke like a dragon. (Revelation 13:11)

This second beast is only a lamb in appearance. When it opens its mouth to speak, it has the voice of a dragon. Its very nature is devilish. We easily recognize the second beast as false religion.[18] It is devotion to man, his kingdoms, his religions, his philosophies and his ideologies. Hence the second beast causes everyone to worship the first beast.

> And he exercises all the authority of the first beast in his presence, and causes the earth and those who dwell in it to worship the first beast, whose deadly wound was healed. He performs great signs, so that he even makes fire come down from heaven on the earth in the sight of men. And he deceives those who dwell on the earth by those signs which he was granted to do in the sight of the beast, telling those who dwell on the earth to make an image to the beast who was wounded by the sword and lived. He was granted power to give breath to the image of the beast, that the image of the beast should both speak . . . (Revelation 13:12–15a)

Great signs are performed to deceive humanity.[19] Note that it is those *who dwell on the earth* who are deceived. Throughout the Revelation, John identifies his believing audience as being in heaven.[20] It is those who are not redeemed by the Lamb who are those who dwell on the earth. In making an image of the beast and giving breath to it, we see the goal of false religion: to deify man, breathing

---

18. The thought compares strongly with Matthew 7:15 and 2 Corinthians 11:13–15, and is to be equated with the false prophet of Revelation 16:13; 19:20; 20:10.

19. Compare also with Mark 13:22; 2 Thessalonians 2:9; and Deuteronomy 13:1–3.

20. Consider Revelation 4:4, 10–11; 5:8–10; 6:9–11; 7:9–10, 13–17; 14:2–5; 15:2–4; 18:20; 21:2, 10.

life into his godlessness, making what is corrupt and decaying seem living and powerful.

> ... and cause as many as would not worship the image of the beast to be killed. He causes all, both small and great, rich and poor, free and slave, to receive a mark on their right hand or on their foreheads, and that no one may buy or sell except one who has the mark or the name of the beast, or the number of his name. (Revelation 13:15b-17)

Let us dive into this passage, because the cashless society holds a prominent place in a lot of popular teaching about the end times.

THE CASHLESS SOCIETY

The introduction of a cashless society is feared by many Christians. Those fears are completely unfounded and based on a misguided approach to the Scripture. Read again the closing verses of Revelation 13.

> He *(the second beast)* causes all, both small and great, rich and poor, free and slave, to receive a mark on their right hand or on their foreheads, and that no one may buy or sell except one who has the mark or the name of the beast, or the number of his name. (Revelation 13:16-17)

In the Revelation, the concept of being marked on the forehead appeared first in chapter 7. There, it was not the ungodly who were marked but believers.[21] Of course, we are not meant to understand this as a literal mark. It symbolizes the seal of ownership and the protection that God places over his children.[22] In the passage above, we now see that unbelievers are also marked.

To understand the symbolism that John is using, we must consider its cultural background. As a young Christian, I often struggled to know what John meant when he talked about people receiving this mark. Why the right hand or forehead? Why not the

---

21. Revelation 7:3. See also Revelation 14:1.
22. Compare with Ephesians 1:13.

left hand? Or an elbow? Or shoulder? Why the forehead? Why not a cheek? Or a chin? Or neck? It just seemed too specific and yet completely arbitrary. And then I learned something important.

For the Hebrew people, the right hand signified a man's strength and was a token of a pledge given in covenant. The forehead represented his thoughts, dreams, and devotion.[23] Remember, the Revelation is peppered with allusions to the Old Testament. John expects us to see the Hebrew idioms in this passage of his Prophetic Drama. The mark on the right hand or forehead signifies that unregenerate man gives his strength and meditations to the gods of his own making, and in so doing, strikes covenant with himself, ultimately to give glory to the god of self.

It is not a literal mark at all. You need not fear Antichrist putting his tattoo on you. In fact, consider the theological absurdities if John meant that the mark was literally placed on people by Antichrist.

- What of the simple Christian who does not know any better and is tricked by Antichrist? Do they lose their salvation—because everyone who receives the mark is thrown into the lake of fire?[24]

- What of the believer with an intellectual disability, whose guardians sanction the receiving of the mark? Do they lose their salvation?

- Perhaps even more to the point, what of the devil worshiper, who enthusiastically and knowingly embraces the mark of the beast? Can they from that moment on never discover the

---

23. Of importance, see Exodus 13:9, 16. The right hand is a prominent idiom of the Hebrew people—see Psalm 16:8; Psalm 98:1; 110:1; Isaiah 41:10, 13; and Jeremiah 22:24. Jacob named his twelfth son, Benjamin, *son of my right hand*. It is also the place where Joseph placed his firstborn to receive Jacob's blessing, Genesis 48:13–18. Mark 14:62; Mark 16:19; Romans 8:34; Hebrews 8:1; and 1 Peter 3:22 show that it was still a prominent idiom in the first century AD. The forehead is not as common, but you will see it in Exodus 28:38 and Ezekiel 3:9.

24. Revelation 14:11.

saving grace of Jesus, particularly when it is one of Christ's hallmarks to save those who are violently opposed to him.[25]

Do you see how shallow is the ground on which the popular teaching about the mark of the beast stands? It robs the gospel of all its power to save. Quite frankly, it is a silly belief.

But here is the sobering truth. Even though there are no physical differences between Christian and non-Christian, they each bear obvious marks. The non-Christian world needs no visible sign to know who to persecute and expel from normal society. The history of the last two thousand years provides ample evidence of the second beast's ability to identify the true worshippers of God. When we talk of persecution, we often think of its extreme examples, when believers are imprisoned and executed for their faith. But this is not the whole story. Usually persecution takes the form of expulsion from regular society, being denied the opportunity to buy and sell.[26]

There is a frightening thought in this. Everyone who does not worship the one true God through active faith in Christ, already bears the mark of the beast. We must be born-again, sealed with God's Holy Spirit, if we are to be rescued.[27] Without Christ, there is nothing to hope for except certain judgment. All non-Christians, wearing the mark of their unbelief, will face God's wrath ... unless God in his mercy causes them to become new creations in Christ.[28] Never forget, before any of us became Christians, we were by nature children of wrath.[29]

---

25. Consider the Apostle Paul, who at one time was overseeing the execution and imprisonment of followers of Christ.

26. Even in societies that do not persecute Christians, believers still regularly miss out on jobs, promotions, or sales simply because of their faith.

27. John 3:3. This is why the Revelation can so universally condemn all who wear the mark of the beast (Revelation 14:9–11, particularly verse 11).

28. 2 Corinthians 5:17.

29. Ephesians 2:3.

ANTICHRIST AND THE BEAST OF JOHN'S REVELATION

Much has been written about Antichrist. In many teachings, Antichrist and John's beast from the sea are synonymous. Now that we have come to learn that the beast is unregenerate humanity in its self-determination, how are we to understand what the Bible says regarding Antichrist?

The word *antichrist* itself only occurs four times in the Bible, all within John's letters. In the first of these, John makes the startling assertion that he was living in the last hour.

> Little children, it is the last hour; and as you have heard that the Antichrist is coming, even now many antichrists have come, by which we know that it is the last hour. (1 John 2:18)

As far as John was concerned, way back in the first century, the lateness of the hour was emphasized by the presence of many Antichrists. The early church was expecting there to be one person who would be the antithesis of everything the Kingdom of God stood for.[30] But John expanded on this. It is not a person (Antichrist) that we should focus on so much as the devilish spirit that lies behind such a one. Till the very end, there will always be many Antichrists, each in his or her own way a personification of the devil's hostility towards God.

In the Greek language, the prefix *anti* can mean *over against, contrary to, in substitution of.* John is saying that Antichrist is anyone who is in opposition to Christ or is a substitute for Christ. More than that, Antichrist is anyone who denies that Jesus is the Christ.

> Who is a liar but he who denies that Jesus is the Christ? He is antichrist[31] who denies the Father and the Son. (1 John 2:22)

---

30. See also 2 Thessalonians 2:3.

31. Interestingly, the Greek text uses the definite article with *antichrist* so the verse reads: "Who is a liar but he who denies that Jesus is the Christ? He is the antichrist who denies the Father and the Son." That changes the feel of John's teaching about Antichrist completely. Anyone can be the Antichrist!

If you stop and think about it, that is an all-encompassing definition. Everyone who is aware of the gospel and has rejected it fits within John's definition of Antichrist. I can think of very few more sobering thoughts. But it most definitely is in keeping with the teaching of the New Testament.[32] How we need the Good News of Jesus, the transforming power of the Spirit, and the love of the Father!

John continues: the Antichrist spirit, long at work in our world, refuses to acknowledge a personal coming of Christ to die on the cross.

> Beloved, do not believe every spirit, but test the spirits, whether they are of God; because many false prophets have gone out into the world. By this you know the Spirit of God: Every spirit that confesses that Jesus Christ has come in the flesh is of God, and every spirit that does not confess that Jesus Christ has come in the flesh is not of God. And this is the spirit of the Antichrist, which you have heard was coming, and is now already in the world. (1 John 4:1–3)

The Antichrist spirit is a lying and deceiving spirit and deceiving doctrines are its language.

> For many deceivers have gone out into the world who do not confess Jesus Christ as coming in the flesh. This is a deceiver and an antichrist. (2 John 7)

I quote the verse from the NKJV. Here again we come across one of those rare occasions when the translators' personal beliefs have influenced their translation. Though in English, the translation uses the indefinite article, *a deceiver* and *an antichrist*, the original language uses the definite article. It literally reads:

> For many deceivers have gone out into the world who do not confess Jesus Christ as coming in the flesh. This is the deceiver and the antichrist. (2 John 7)

Now, it is not technically wrong for the translators to use the indefinite article. As we have noted earlier in our studies, New

---

32. Ephesians 2:2b.

Testament Greek is different to English in how it uses the definite article, *the*. But you can see how radically 2 John 7 changes when we draw attention to John's use of the definite article. "Many deceivers have gone out." "This is the deceiver and the antichrist." It is obvious that John does not want us to think that there is going to be one, specific, all-powerful Antichrist.

Because the spirit of Antichrist may not immediately be obvious, John warns us that the spirits need to be tested. Our adversary may be disguised as an angel of light and it is precisely this thought that is expressed in Paul's writings.[33]

Over the centuries, there have been many claims of this person or that system being Antichrist. These may well have been accurate, identifying manifestations in their generation of the spirit of Antichrist. So, Nero of the first century was Antichrist. So too was the medieval papacy, Stalin, Hitler, Mao, Hussein. The error is in ascribing to one particular person the prophecy's absolute fulfilment.

In fact, the final Antichrist most likely will not be quickly discerned. And he may not necessarily be distinguishable from those who have preceded him, merely the last iteration of the Antichrist spirit.

Many beliefs of Eschatology link Antichrist with the beast of Revelation, but it should be obvious by now that the two are not at all the same. As we have seen, the beast is man, living outside God's righteous rule. Antichrist is an embodiment of this for sure. The spirit that empowers Antichrist is the same spirit that is at work in all people and in that sense, the spirit of Antichrist is the spirit of the Beast. However, the beast is unregenerate man in general, whereas the Antichrist refers to individual people or systems within the mass of unregenerate humanity.

THE MAN OF LAWLESSNESS

In relation to our discussion concerning Antichrist, 2 Thessalonians 2 is full of intrigue and warrants specific attention.

---

33. See 2 Corinthians 11:14 and 2 Thessalonians 2:4.

> Now, brethren, concerning the coming of our Lord Jesus Christ and our gathering together to Him, we ask you, not to be soon shaken in mind or troubled, either by spirit or by word or by letter, as if from us, as though the day of Christ had come. Let no one deceive you by any means; for that Day will not come unless the falling away comes first, and the man of sin is revealed, the son of perdition, who opposes and exalts himself above all that is called God or that is worshiped, so that he sits as God in the temple of God, showing himself that he is God. (2 Thessalonians 2:1–4)

Before Jesus returns, the man of lawlessness must be revealed. Paul expected a literal identity. Indeed, the whole church did.[34] As we have already seen, however, John broadened this belief. This spirit of Antichrist has been displayed in many people and systems throughout the centuries. It is apparent, however, that Paul talks of the final manifestation of that spirit in reference to the man of lawlessness.

This person sets himself up above everything that is to be worshipped or called God. We see in this an enactment of Satan's own sin.[35] He even claims deity! This final manifestation of the Antichrist spirit will come from within the temple of God. No matter what you have heard in the past, we are not meant to look for a rebuilding of the Jewish temple in Jerusalem. The temple Paul talks of is the church. This is easily shown by considering how the New Testament uses the two Greek words that translate as *temple*.

The first Greek word is *hieron*. It is used seventy-one times in the New Testament and only ever refers to a physical structure, built in honor of a deity, where worship and sacrifice are performed.[36]

The other Greek word translated as *temple* in the New Testament is *naos*. It relates to the inner edifice of a temple, typically

---

34. Compare with 1 John 2:18.
35. Compare with Isaiah 14:12–14.
36. In the New Testament, the word typically refers to the Jewish temple in Jerusalem, but it was used more broadly than that in the Greek speaking world of the first century. Consider Acts 19:27 where it refers to the Temple of Artemis in Ephesus.

where the statue of the deity stood. The word is used extensively in the Septuagint translation of the Old Testament depicting the sanctuary itself rather that the entire temple precinct. It is used forty-six times in the New Testament in the following ways...

In the Gospels/Acts, *naos* appears twenty-two times.

- Referring specifically to the then temple—fourteen times.[37]
- A reference to pagan temples and shrines—two times.[38]
- Jesus' body that would die on the cross and be raised again—six times.[39]

The Revelation uses *naos* sixteen times. We need not investigate these, given that the book has an overt leaning towards symbolism and that will not instruct us as to how to read Paul in 2 Thessalonians 2.

Paul, in his epistles, uses *naos* eight times.

- Referring specifically to the church—six times.[40]
- Referring to the individual believer—one time.[41]
- And the verse we are looking at, 2 Thessalonians 2:4, concerning the man of sin.

If we just looked at a surface level on the New Testament, and only took into account total occurrences of the word without considering their contexts, we might end up concluding that *naos* in 2 Thessalonians 2:4 could well be referring to the temple in Jerusalem.

---

37. Matthew 23:16 (2x), 17, 21, 35; 27:5, 51; Mark 15:38; Luke 1:9, 21, 22; 23:45; John 2:20; Acts 7:48.

38. Acts 17:24; 19:24.

39. Matthew 26:61; 27:40; Mark 14:58; 15:29; John 2:19, 21.

40. 1 Corinthians 3:16, 17 (2x); 2 Corinthians 6:16 (2x); Ephesians 2:21.

41. 1 Corinthians 6:19. Because our English language does not differentiate between you (singular) and you (plural), it is easy to misrepresent Paul's revelation. Yes, the individual believer is a temple of the Holy Spirit, but that is only stated once, here in 1 Corinthians 6:19. The gathering of God's people, however, as either the local or universal church, is emphatically declared six times to be the temple of the Holy Spirit. In our highly individualistic society, this is a call for family.

But we have just now seen that individual authors use the word very specifically. In particular, Paul uses it to depict his revelation of the New Testament church. It would be extraordinary for him, in our passage in 2 Thessalonians, to break from that and expect his readers to see anything other than the church.

Let me put it plainly: there is no prophetic expectation for a physical temple to be reestablished in modern-day Jerusalem.[42] Regarding the man of sin, Paul went on to declare that something was presently holding him back.

> And now you know what is restraining, that he may be revealed in his own time. (2 Thessalonians 2:6)

The final Antichrist cannot come at any time other than that appointed him by God himself. The devil does not determine the times—all things are under the Father's control.

> For the mystery of lawlessness is already at work; only He who now restrains will do so until He is taken out of the way. (2 Thessalonians 2:7)

The quote is from the NKJV, which uniformly capitalizes personal pronouns that relate to God. So we have "He who now restrains," meaning it is the Lord who is restraining the working of lawlessness. This is an appropriate ascribing of the pronoun, *he*, to God. Though there are many Antichrists, and the spirit of Antichrist is at work in our world, its power is held back by God from achieving its full potential.

The second use of *he* in the passage, however, is a little awkward. " . . . until He is taken out of the way . . . " It is much more contextually satisfying to have this referring to the man of lawlessness. Do we really expect God himself to be taken out of the way? I do not think so. The NKJV translators should have left the second *he* without a capital.

> For the mystery of lawlessness is already at work; only He who now restrains will do so until he *(the man of sin)* is taken out of the way. (2 Thessalonians 2:7)

---

42. I will expand this very shortly when we discuss Ezekiel's prophetic vision of the temple.

What the passage teaches us is that the devil's power to unreservedly act in defiance against God is restrained. The church is a potent force in our world, and the devil most assuredly wants it overthrown, but he has been prevented from eradicating God's people. Although the mystery of lawlessness is at work in our world, it is not lord of its destiny.

> And then the lawless one will be revealed, whom the Lord will consume with the breath of His mouth and destroy with the brightness of His coming. (2 Thessalonians 2:8)

Antichrist will be overthrown by the breath of Jesus' mouth, the Word of his authority. In fact, his overthrow will be so easily accomplished that the mere presence of Christ will destroy him.

Before that time though, the lawless one will come with a deceptive display of signs and wonders.

> The coming of the lawless one is according to the working of Satan, with all power, signs, and lying wonders, and with all unrighteous deception among those who perish, because they did not receive the love of the truth, that they might be saved. (2 Thessalonians 2:9–10)

I have heard many Christians worry over this passage, concerned that a genuine gift of the Spirit may be a deception of the devil and that believers could unwittingly buy into the man of lawlessness's lie. This is not at all what the Scripture is saying. The deception is among those who perish. And why do they perish? Because they do not take hold of the truth of the gospel.

We need to embrace this firmly in our hearts. We are saved by grace through faith. We are not saved because we are smart and perceptively see through the veiled lies of the enemy. That would mean that gullible Christians are at risk of aligning themselves with the devil. It would mean that the gospel has the power to save us, but not the power to keep and protect us. It would mean that the Holy Spirit is at work in our salvation, but far from us in our day to day living.

The passage we are studying states clearly that those who are deceived are those who do not love the truth. That is not you if you have given your life to Jesus. If you love the truth—and Jesus is the Truth—you cannot be deceived by these so-called signs and wonders. They will be obvious.

> But we are bound to give thanks to God always for you, brethren beloved by the Lord, because God from the beginning chose you for salvation through sanctification by the Spirit and belief in the truth, to which He called you by our gospel, for the obtaining of the glory of our Lord Jesus Christ. Therefore, brethren, stand fast and hold the traditions which you were taught, whether by word or our epistle. (2 Thessalonians 2:13-15)

The whole impact of Paul's treatment of Christ's return in 2 Thessalonians is that the coming of the Lord will be obvious and, though there may be periods of testing, salvation will appear for all who love the truth. The victory of Christ resounds throughout all time.

EZEKIEL'S TEMPLE

Because of the widespread belief in Dispensationalism, Christians all over the world expect that one day the temple will be rebuilt in Jerusalem. Given that the Islamic Dome of the Rock currently stands on the temple mount, it is believed that only a war of Armageddon proportions could result in the destruction of that edifice in order to pave the way for the rebuilding of the temple.

But is that what the Scripture says? We have already seen that a rebuilt temple was not in Paul's thinking when he described the man of lawlessness in 2 Thessalonians 2. But what of Ezekiel's temple? It has never been built.

And it never will be, not as a literal structure at least. Let me show you.

In chapter 4, *Uncovering the Apocalypse*, we looked in detail at John's vision of the heavenly city, the New Jerusalem. We saw how stunning a picture of the New Testament church that vision declared us to be a part of. And we noted that John alluded to Ezekiel's

The Lost Message of the End Times

vision of the temple and its surrounds. The two visions ought to be read together.

- John's New Jerusalem, like Ezekiel's rebuilt Jerusalem, is marked with the Presence of God.[43]
- John's New Jerusalem, like Ezekiel's rebuilt temple, has a river flowing from God's throne.[44]
- On either side of the river is the tree of life, whose leaves are for the healing of the nations.[45]

To my mind, there is enough in those three comparisons to show that Ezekiel's prophecy is very similar to John's and can rightly be interpreted as an Old Testament vision of the glories of the New Testament church. And, in fact, it must be so. If we were to think that Ezekiel was talking of a real temple, its physical dimensions would simply defy reason.

> He measured it on the four sides; it had a wall all around, five hundred cubits[46] long and five hundred wide, to separate the holy areas from the common. Ezekiel 42:20

The dimensions of the outer court of the temple are approximately four times the size of the entire city of Jerusalem as it was in Ezekiel's day. More to the point, it is over fifty times the size of Old Jerusalem, the City of David, which contains the temple mount. Solomon's Temple, destroyed by the Babylonians in 586BC not long before Ezekiel prophesied, covered only one acre of land. Given that Ezekiel's temple is a mile square, you can easily see that it cannot possibly be contained on Mount Zion, and inside Jerusalem.

---

43. Revelation 21:3 compares with Ezekiel 48:35.
44. Revelation 22:1 compares with Ezekiel 47:1.
45. Revelation 22:2 compares with Ezekiel 47:12.
46. The word *cubit* is not in the Hebrew text of Ezekiel 42:20. It is curious that the NKJV translators used it, because throughout the passage the word *rod* was used. That *rod* was defined in the beginning of the vision as a *long cubit*, being a cubit and a handbreadth, which is twenty-one inches, as opposed to the standard cubit of eighteen inches. Thus, this outer court was almost exactly one mile square.

Around the temple is an area set apart as most holy.[47]

> The entire district shall be twenty-five thousand cubits[48] by twenty-five thousand cubits, four square. You shall set apart the holy district with the property of the city.
> Ezekiel 48:20

The dimensions do not fit the geographical boundaries that Ezekiel demanded. Ezekiel 47:18 told that the land was bordered on the west by the Mediterranean Sea and on the east by the Jordan River. But the dimensions we have just cited above, a square of approximately fifty miles cannot fit within those limits. It is too big. The distance of the Mediterranean coast to the Jordan varies considerably, but only in the far south is there at least fifty miles between the two. In places, it is less than forty. To fit such a neat square within the topography, either the Mediterranean or the Jordan has to move.

Ezekiel 47 describes the river that flows from under the very threshold of the temple towards the east.

> Then he said to me: "This water flows toward the eastern region, goes down into the valley, and enters the sea. When it reaches the sea, its waters are healed."
> Ezekiel 47:8

Given the terrain, such a river cannot flow east, nor indeed is it likely that such a river should spring forth from the top of a mountain, let alone that spring grow into a torrent within the space of four thousand cubits,[49] just over a mile, without a multitude of tributaries feeding it.

We can definitely conclude that Ezekiel's vision does not have a literal application. Yet because the popular Dispensational view of Eschatology is widely accepted, which sees war in the Middle East and the rising of the Antichrist in a rebuilt temple in Jerusalem, it is

---

47. Ezekiel 48:9–20.
48. Remember, this is the long cubit of twenty-one inches, not eighteen inches.
49. Ezekiel 47:3–5.

commonly taught that this is what Ezekiel was prophesying about. We can easily see, however, that he was not.

In fact, if it was to be rebuilt, it would in no way be under the direction of God, as it would require him to sanction the re-introduction of the rituals and sacrifices of the old covenant. Yet, the physical temple, along with its attendant worship, was always a shadow of things to come. As Paul says, the shadow no longer has a place when the reality has come.

> So let no one judge you in food or in drink, or regarding a festival or a new moon or sabbaths, which are a shadow of things to come, but the substance is of Christ. (Colossians 2:16–17)

Obviously, if the temple was to be rebuilt on the temple mount, the sacred Muslim shrine, the Dome of the Rock, would have to be demolished, along with the al-Aqsa Mosque which stands on what used to be the temple courtyard. And yes, if that happened, our world would have a war of Biblical proportions on its hands. But let me be emphatic, there is nothing in Scripture that says that this will happen. No prophecy relates to such an event. Ezekiel did not talk about it. His prophecy spoke of the glories of the church that the Messiah would establish at his first coming. It speaks of the river of life that flows freely to all who thirst. The Lord himself is present within its holy borders.

The expectation that the temple will be rebuilt in Jerusalem is faulty. Jesus could come back right now even though the Dome of the Rock still features in Jerusalem's skyline.

THE GREAT APOSTASY IN THE LAST DAYS

In his second letter to Timothy, Paul instructed the young pastor of the church at Ephesus.

> But know this, that in the last days perilous times will come: For men will be lovers of themselves, lovers of money, boasters, proud, blasphemers, disobedient to parents, unthankful, unholy, unloving, unforgiving, slanderers, without self-control, brutal, despisers of

good, traitors, headstrong, haughty, lovers of pleasure rather than lovers of God, having a form of godliness but denying its power. And from such people turn away! (2 Timothy 3:1–5)

Paul was not referring to some future time in this passage. "From such people turn away!" He understood himself to be living in the last days.[50] Here, he simply drew Timothy's attention to the fact that godlessness will accompany these times, hence his command to have nothing to do with such people. In his letter, he instructed Timothy how to deal with what was a present problem. In doing so, he warns us all of the lateness of the hour.

> Nevertheless, God's solid foundation stands firm, sealed with this inscription: "The Lord knows those who are his" and "Everyone who confesses the name of the Lord must turn away from wickedness."
>
> 2 TIMOTHY 2:19

---

50. Compare with 1 Corinthians 10:11 "Now all these things happened to them as examples, and they were written for our admonition, upon whom the ends of the ages have come."

8

Prophetic Times

OUR INVESTIGATION OF THE great themes of Eschatology is not complete without discussing the role that specific time periods play in the unfolding of God's word to us. Seventy weeks; one thousand years; forty-two months; twelve hundred and sixty days; three and a half years or days; and times, times, and half a time. These all make their way into the end times discussion. What are we to make of these mysterious times?

THE TIMEFRAMES OF JOHN'S REVELATION

Amongst the symbolism and allusions of the Revelation, time has an important place. We have already studied the significance of the one thousand year reign of Christ, the millennium. But there are other times that feature even more prominently than the thousand years.

> But leave out the court which is outside the temple, and do not measure it, for it has been given to the Gentiles. And they will tread the holy city underfoot for forty-two months. And I will give power to my two witnesses, and they will prophesy one thousand two hundred and sixty days, clothed in sackcloth. (Revelation 11:2–3)

Prophetic Times

We have already studied the vision of the two witnesses in chapter 5, *The War of Armageddon*, but I did not dive into the significance of the depicted timeframes. We will consider it now.

First of all, note the close association in the passage above of the two time periods, forty-two months and one thousand two hundred and sixty days. You probably will not be surprised to learn that the Jewish calendar that John was familiar with is not the same as the Gregorian calendar that we use today. Our months vary in length, with an additional day added every leap year. The calendar John used consisted of twelve months of thirty days each.[1] Forty-two months, each of thirty days, is one thousand two hundred and sixty days. In other words, the time for the trampling of the holy city by the Gentiles is the same as the time for the prophesying of the two witnesses.

We see this again in the next chapter of the Revelation when John painted a picture of the devil's pursuit of the people of God.

> Then the woman fled into the wilderness, where she has a place prepared by God, that they should feed her there one thousand two hundred and sixty days. (Revelation 12:6)

> But the woman was given two wings of a great eagle, that she might fly into the wilderness to her place, where she is nourished for a time and times and half a time, from the presence of the serpent. (Revelation 12:14)

We see here again the one thousand two hundred and sixty days and also note that they are equated with the curiously phrased time and times and half a time. John, in this, is clearly alluding to Daniel's prophecies.

> He shall speak pompous words against the Most High, shall persecute the saints of the Most High, and shall intend to change times and law. Then the saints shall be given into his hand for a time and times and half a time. (Daniel 7:25)

---

1. They had their own version of a leap year, by periodically adding a thirteenth month.

Both this passage, and another like it—Daniel 12:7, feature within Daniel's prophecy of the four world empires that would rise in the world preceding the first coming of Christ. Those empires were the Babylonian, Persian, Greek, and Roman Empires. We discussed these in chapter 7, *The Mark of the Beast*. Of note, the two verses in which Daniel uses the expression times, times, and half a time feature in his prophecy concerning the Roman Empire.

Earlier in Daniel,[2] the prophet interpreted a dream of Nebuchadnezzar's that concerned seven times, a period that was understood to be seven years. With that as the background to Daniel's later prophecies, we gain insight into what is meant by the mysterious time and times and half a time. Think in terms of one time, two times, and half a time to better understand the expression. Time and times and half a time is three and a half times. Or three and a half years. It is half of seven times. That will soon become important for us.

Coming back to John's Revelation, we see the numbers now starting to come into alignment. One thousand two hundred and sixty days equals forty-two months equals three and a half years equals time and times and half a time. The same time is given for the trampling of the church by the world,[3] the prophesying of the two witnesses,[4] the woman's stay in the wilderness,[5] and the beast's authority.[6]

Given John's overt use of allusion to the Old Testament, we cannot go past the three and a half year drought invoked by Elijah in the time of Ahab.[7] We could probably leave it there and conclude that these times show that God is in charge, that he nurtures his own people while warning their world of impending judgment. And this is certainly what the numbers are telling us. But historically, those same numbers keep cropping up. Antiochus Epiphanes'

2. See Daniel 4:16.
3. Revelation 11:2.
4. Revelation 11:3.
5. Revelation 12:6, 14.
6. Revelation 13:6.
7. Refer to Luke 4:25; James 5:17.

second century BC war against Jerusalem and sacking of the temple lasted about three and a half years; the first century AD Roman conflict in the Jerusalem riots culminating in the destruction of the temple also lasted about three and a half years; the children of Israel made forty-two camps in their wilderness wanderings.[8] The point is, being in charge of the destinies of all people of all time, God has painted elaborate pictures of ultimate reality within our very history.

Of course, none of these timeframes are meant to be taken literally. To emphasize this, John incorporates Daniel's non-specific *time, times, and half a time*. No actual chronological period (hour, day, month, or year) is meant at all. Three and a half times is half of seven times and relates to the divine seven, with an emphatic reminder of the divine judgment in Elijah's day. This is how we are to understand all related timeframes—forty-two months, one thousand two hundred and sixty days, three and a half years, and also the three and a half days in Revelation 11:9.

DANIEL'S SEVENTY WEEKS AND THE COMING OF CHRIST

Amongst Daniel's fascinating prophecies is the amazing prediction concerning the seventy weeks that lead to the coming of the Anointed One. It is an important prophecy and holds a prominent place in many views of Eschatology.

> Seventy weeks are determined for your people and for your holy city, to finish the transgression, to make an end of sins, to make reconciliation for iniquity, to bring in everlasting righteousness, to seal up vision and prophecy, and to anoint the Most Holy. (Daniel 9:24)

The seventy weeks, or seventy *sevens* as it reads in some versions of the Bible,[9] are not to be understood as being literal weeks, i.e. just under a year and a half. As we will shortly see, the events

---

8. Refer to Numbers 33:5–49.
9. In Hebrew, the words *seven* and *week* are the same.

mentioned in the very next verse could not be fulfilled in such a short space of time. Many teachers of Eschatology hold that the seventy weeks prophetically indicate seventy weeks of years. Accordingly, the seventy weeks would represent 490 years. Because it is commonly taught this way, we will look at it closely to see if that is a valid interpretation.

Verse 24 that we have just read stated that seventy weeks were decreed for Daniel's people and his holy city. By the completion of the seventy weeks, six things would have occurred.

- transgressions finished
- sin put to an end
- atonement made for wickedness
- bring in everlasting righteousness
- seal up vision and prophecy
- anoint the most holy[10]

The prophecy then goes on to describe these weeks, dividing them into three periods, commencing with the issuing of the decree to restore and rebuild Jerusalem.

> Know therefore and understand, that from the going forth of the command to restore and build Jerusalem until Messiah the Prince, there shall be seven weeks and sixty-two weeks; the street shall be built again, and the wall, even in troublesome times. (Daniel 9:25)

Some maintain this decree was issued by the Persian king, Cyrus, in 536BC.[11] Others favor an order given by Artaxerxes 1 in 457BC.[12] Within the context of the prophecy, however, we encounter two significant problems.

---

10. These all reflect the ministry and work of Christ on the cross. Compare with Isaiah 53:5-8 and Isaiah 44:22. See also Hebrews 9:26; 2 Corinthians 5:21; Acts 3:18; and Luke 4:17-21.

11. Ezra 1:2-4.

12. Nehemiah 2:1-9. The date of Artaxerxes is often preferred because four hundred and ninety years after 457BC is 34AD. The prophecy would therefore culminate around the time of Christ.

The first difficulty arises from the silence of the New Testament with respect to the whole passage. If, indeed, it gives a specific timeframe that would have enabled Daniel and his contemporaries to predetermine the dates surrounding Christ's life and ministry,[13] it would be paramount amongst fulfilled Messianic prophecy. Yet the New Testament, which leans heavily on the Old Testament to substantiate Christ's claims, omits this prophecy of Daniel's altogether!

This embarrassing silence shows that neither Jesus nor the apostles understood Daniel 9 as giving a timeframe for Christ's arrival. As we come to interpret the passage, we must account for this silence of the New Testament.

The second problem is that Artaxerxes did not issue the decree that Daniel predicted. Under Medo-Persian law, a decree was never repealed. Artaxerxes, in sending Nehemiah to rebuild Jerusalem, was not issuing a new decree, but rather enforcing the decree of Cyrus some eighty years earlier. It is understood that the passage recorded in Ezra 1:2–4 only specifies the building of the temple, but it is implicit, at least as far as Artaxerxes was concerned, and indeed as far as the prophet Isaiah was also concerned,[14] that this included the complete rebuilding of Jerusalem. Hence, when Artaxerxes sent Nehemiah to Jerusalem, he did not enact a decree as Cyrus had done.[15]

Of course, if 457 BC is rejected as a starting point, this leaves us with Cyrus's 536 BC date. Unfortunately, four hundred and ninety years after this does not leave us anywhere near Christ's time, but places us in the middle of the first century BC.

Now, we need to note that the word Messiah does not necessarily have to refer to Jesus. Israelite kings and priests were all inducted into office with ceremonial anointing oil and were therefore regarded as ones that have been anointed, i.e. anointed ones, or in the Hebrew tongue, *messiahs*.

Over the centuries, not all commentators have agreed that Daniel's prophecy relates to Jesus. Enough historical evidence has

---

13. A belief popular in Dispensationalism and Historical Premillennialism.
14. Isaiah 44:28.
15. Compare the much looser wording of Nehemiah 2:1–9 with Ezra 1:2–4.

been furnished to support an argument for fulfilment outside of Christ. Taking the arrival of this *messiah* to be sixty-nine weeks (four hundred and eighty-three years) after Cyrus' decree in 536 BC, we are left with a date around 53 BC. For sure, that is a significant date, because it was around that time that the Roman Governor, Crassus,[16] plundered the temple in Jerusalem. That is not to suggest he was a messiah figure, but the plundering of the temple that he instigated can arguably identify him as a candidate for the "one who makes desolate" in the closing verses of the prophecy.[17] Certainly, in taking this as the preferred interpretation, the two problems we have been considering are quickly eliminated.

Nevertheless, verse 24 does give prophetic insight into Jesus' ministry, and it is hard to read the passage apart from fulfilment in Christ. How then are we to understand the seventy weeks, because the numbers just do not add up?

Our problem is that we take Biblical prophecy literally, even when we know it is laden with metaphors and imagery. Seventy sevens is an interesting number in and of itself, and seven features heavily in prophetic announcements. Although the passage is commonly regarded as indicating four hundred and ninety actual years, a symbolic interpretation is to be favored. It allows for the starting date being in the time of Cyrus, accounts for the silence of the New Testament, and acknowledges the obvious reference to Christ who was not four hundred and ninety years after Cyrus.

If you have been thoroughly schooled in popular Eschatology, it might seem to you that taking a symbolic approach to Daniel's seventy weeks is drawing too much of a long straw. But keep Daniel's actual language in focus. His word for week is *seven*. The prophecy spoke of seventy sevens. We are looking at a Jewish idiom here. Consider, by way of example, the question that was posed to Jesus about how often we should forgive a brother.

> Then Peter came to Him and said, "Lord, how often shall my brother sin against me, and I forgive him? Up to

---

16. Crassus was successor to the Roman General, Pompey, who was responsible for making Judea a Roman tributary.

17. Daniel 9:26–27.

seven times?" Jesus said to him, "I do not say to you, up
to seven times, but up to seventy times seven." (Matthew
18:21–22)

Neither Peter nor Jesus were speaking of specific numbers. Peter used the Hebrew idiomatic *seven* to indicate a number that would meet the divine expectation. He was not wanting to get off the hook, so to speak, if his brother sinned against him eight times. Jesus understood this, but in his reply went over the top to indicate how extreme God's demand for us to be forgiving is. Seven times does not describe the heart posture of one who has been forgiven by God himself. Seventy times seven is a more fitting number for Jesus. Of course, he is not meaning that if your brother sinned against you more than four hundred and ninety times, you are free to hold his offense against him. That is easy to see. Jesus' response shows the importance of numbers in Jewish idioms.

Allow me to paraphrase Matthew 18:22.

Jesus said to him, "Seven times? Do you think that is
all the Father cares about? I say, not seven, but seventy
sevens is how many times you must forgive." (Matthew
18:22, my paraphrase)

Seventy sevens—the equivalent of what was declared in Daniel's prophecy for the time to the Messiah. It is not a pedantic number. It indicates a long time, but one that God is totally in control of. At just the right time, the Messiah will come.

These seventy sevens, or weeks, are broken into three timeframes, the first and last being of prime importance as shown in the following diagram.

The first block consists of seven sevens and indicates the commencement of God's plan for Jerusalem and his people, depicting the restoration of the city and temple. And as the prophecy predicted, Jerusalem was certainly rebuilt in times of trouble.[18]

The last seven is the time period surrounding the ministry and passion of Christ. It is not a literal seven years but merely denotes the divine ministry of Christ which has the crucifixion at its focal point. The period of sixty-two sevens simply indicates a long period of time and is employed by Daniel to complete the numerical total of seventy sevens.

A hotly debated portion of Daniel's prophecy is the second half of verse 26, concerning the people of the ruler who will come.

> And after the sixty-two weeks Messiah shall be cut off, but not for Himself; and the people of the prince who is to come shall destroy the city and the sanctuary. The end of it shall be with a flood, and till the end of the war desolations are determined. Then he[19] shall confirm a covenant with many for one week; but in the middle of the week He shall bring an end to sacrifice and offering. And on the wing of abominations shall be one who makes desolate, even until the consummation, which is determined, is poured out on the desolate. (Daniel 9:26–27)

---

18. Refer to the book of Nehemiah, which describes the events of the restoration of Jerusalem.

19. Note the use of the lower case *he*. This reveals the NKJV translators' understanding of Eschatology—they do not believe it relates to the Messiah.

It is easiest, and most consistent with New Testament teaching, if brackets are placed around the second half of verse 26.

> And after the sixty-two weeks Messiah shall be cut off, but not for Himself. (And the people of the prince who is to come shall destroy the city and the sanctuary. The end of it shall be with a flood, and till the end of the war desolations are determined.) Then He shall confirm a covenant . . .

By placing the brackets where I have, it is easy to see that the "one who confirms the covenant with many" is the Messiah who would be "cut off." In other words, the *he* needs to be *He*. The last seven finds its fulfilment in Jesus' earthly ministry, culminating in his crucifixion where he put an end, once and for all, to the Mosaic law of sacrifice and offering.[20]

The remaining question to be answered is: Who are the people of the prince to come? When do/did they come? Note that the city would be destroyed by the people of the prince to come, not by that prince himself. The prince to come is often identified as the little horn of Daniel's fourth beast, the Roman Empire. A popular contemporary belief sees this as a reference to Antichrist, but it is too easy to recognize this part of the prophecy as being fulfilled by the Romans, beginning in 70AD with the destruction of the temple, and culminating in 120AD when the city was finally destroyed.

"On the wing of abominations shall be one who makes desolate" undoubtedly refers to the desecration of the temple which occurred in 70AD.[21]

Amazingly then, and despite the way this passage gains central importance in popular preaching, we discover that it provides no anticipation of the Second Coming at all! Rather, it finds its complete fulfilment in Jesus' First Coming, his life and death, and in

---

20. Daniel notes that after the 62 weeks, sometime in the last week, the Messiah will be cut off. Compare with the language Isaiah incorporates when discussing the crucifixion of Christ. "He was taken from prison and from judgment, and who will declare His generation? For He was cut off from the land of the living; for the transgressions of My people He was stricken." (Isaiah 53:8).

21. Refer to our previous discussion on the Olivet Discourse in chapter 3, *Signs of the Times*.

the destruction of the Jewish temple and Jerusalem in the first and second centuries AD.

ETERNITY FROM ISAIAH'S PERSPECTIVE

We will conclude this chapter with Isaiah's best-known vision of eternity, found in Isaiah 65. It forms an intriguing study of the millennial age because it poses a problem that all views of Eschatology must address.

> "For behold, I create new heavens and a new earth; and the former shall not be remembered or come to mind. But be glad and rejoice forever in what I create; for behold, I create Jerusalem as a rejoicing, and her people a joy. I will rejoice in Jerusalem, and joy in My people; the voice of weeping shall no longer be heard in her, nor the voice of crying. No more shall an infant from there live but a few days, nor an old man who has not fulfilled his days; for the child shall die one hundred years old, but the sinner being one hundred years old shall be accursed. They shall build houses and inhabit them; they shall plant vineyards and eat their fruit. They shall not build and another inhabit; they shall not plant and another eat; for as the days of a tree, so shall be the days of My people, and My elect shall long enjoy the work of their hands. They shall not labor in vain, nor bring forth children for trouble; for they shall be the descendants of the blessed of the LORD, and their offspring with them. It shall come to pass that before they call, I will answer; and while they are still speaking, I will hear. The wolf and the lamb shall feed together, the lion shall eat straw like the ox, and dust shall be the serpent's food. They shall not hurt nor destroy in all My holy mountain," says the LORD. (Isaiah 65:17-25)

In the passage, we see people living to extreme old age and carnivores becoming herbivorous. It seems reminiscent of the pre-Noahic world, a time when the Earth was young and pristine. So premillennialists often interpret the text as referring to the thousand years after Christ's return. They expect that after such a long time with Jesus as the global leader, much of the idyllic past will have been recaptured. Their problem is that the creation of the new heavens and new earth begins this prophecy. For premillennialists, this happens after their millennial reign of Christ, not before. It comes about from too literal a reading of Bible prophecy.

Let me paint a new picture for you, a vision of a time that we are stepping into collectively as the royal priesthood of believers. This passage talks of both the future and the present. The whole of the Old Testament looked forward to the coming of Christ. And the whole of the New Testament looks back on that same time. It is all about Jesus. He is the focal point of God's narrative, the crux of history.

Now, because we are in him, when we look back to the cross, we see our own crucifixion. In his resurrection, we see a foretaste of our own. In his sitting at the right hand of the Father, we see our own position in the heavens. You see, Christ is the firstfruits. His story has become ours. We are the new creation. We have the seeds of that new world within us, the firstfruits of the Spirit. Our citizenship is above. Our Kingdom is not of this world. In short, we are people of the future, living in the present.

This prophecy of Isaiah's shows us God's dream for his people, that they would understand who they are, that they would live in intimate union with God himself. Jesus is our Forerunner. He has given us a clear vision of what happens when a Man in beautiful, consecrated union with the Father, knowing his identity as a Son, walks about in our fallen world. Healings are manifest at even the touch of a garment. Thousands are impossibly fed despite overwhelming lack. The ordinary is transformed into the luxurious. The physical elements themselves are enthralled, obedient to his command.

Take note! Jesus is the firstfruits. We are in him. We have the gift of his Spirit that attests to our identity as sons. He has commissioned us with the commission he himself was charged with. We are told to heal the sick, to be clothed with power from on high. Can you see it? When men and women truly see themselves as people of the future, they walk differently. They pray differently. They have different expectations. They carry a presence. They influence the world around them.

Look again at Isaiah's vision. YHWH, the covenant making God, declares that he creates new heavens and a new earth. He is the Creator. Right now, he is remodeling, reordering, redeeming. He did not simply send his Son to redeem our souls. His blood paid for the redemption of the whole creation.

The creation is desperate for you and me to apprehend what it is that Christ purchased for us.

> For the earnest expectation of the creation eagerly waits for the revealing of the sons of God. (Romans 8:19)

That revealing, of course, will be complete and ultimate when Christ returns.

> Beloved, now we are children of God; and it has not yet been revealed what we shall be, but we know that when He is revealed, we shall be like Him, for we shall see Him as He is. (1 John 3:2)

But that does not mean that we sit back and wait for the glories to come. We are people of the future, so we bring that future into the present. The creation around us is renewed as we daily gain revelation of what it is that God has done for us in Christ, of who we are in him, of how all-encompassing his death on the cross was for all eternity.

Our sonship needs to be revealed to us. We cannot go back to old rules and regulations, having the form of faith but not the substance. Law does not redeem our world. It is when sons and daughters discover who they are, and the authority and power they are clothed with, that they start to walk as Jesus did. And the rocks and stones themselves will cry out in praise.

> For behold, I create new heavens and a new earth; and the former shall not be remembered or come to mind. But be glad and rejoice forever in what I create; for behold, I create Jerusalem as a rejoicing, and her people a joy. I will rejoice in Jerusalem, and joy in My people; the

> voice of weeping shall no longer be heard in her, nor the voice of crying. (Isaiah 65:17–19)

This is who we are. The former things are insignificant, so great is the glory that Christ invites us into.[22] Where there was sorrow and weeping, the tender affection of our Savior has wiped away our tears. Wonder has replaced our mourning. Jerusalem, the Old Testament image of the church, the Bride of Christ, is filled with rejoicing! That is who we are. Filled with a Joy that cannot be contained.

> No more shall an infant from there live but a few days, nor an old man who has not fulfilled his days; for the child shall die one hundred years old, but the sinner being one hundred years old shall be accursed. They shall build houses and inhabit them; they shall plant vineyards and eat their fruit. They shall not build and another inhabit; they shall not plant and another eat; for as the days of a tree, so shall be the days of My people, and My elect shall long enjoy the work of their hands. They shall not labor in vain, nor bring forth children for trouble; for they shall be the descendants of the blessed of the LORD, and their offspring with them. (Isaiah 65:20–23)

Isaiah, looking through the prophetic telescope to the future glories of the church, sees a time when the Kingdom has overtaken the world. The Father has already instructed Christ to sit at his right hand until he places all his enemies under his feet. The last enemy is death, and we have already spoken at length about that. Death is destroyed at the resurrection. But this vision of Isaiah's tells of the time leading up to that last enemy's subjection.

---

22. The Hebrew use of language is relationally charged. The word *remember* does not mean the same for Isaiah as it does for us. When Isaiah heard YHWH saying the former shall not be remembered, he understood that God was saying that it would not come into play regarding the new thing God was doing. This is important to know. You are not defined by your past. The former shall not be remembered. That is not to say that God does not recall the facts of your personal history. What it is saying is that those facts will have no bearing over how God treats you today. All things are new.

In that vision, death has not been defeated, but lifespans are greatly lengthened. It is a time when Jerusalem, the church, has truly realized who they are. The world under their influence, and subject to their heaven-stamped stewardship, is a world that prospers. Children are not born into a world of conflict and despair. They will be the descendants of the blessed of YHWH, and that blessing will flow to their generations.

> It shall come to pass that before they call, I will answer; and while they are still speaking, I will hear. (Isaiah 65:24)

This is our inheritance right now if we would receive it. He is not a Father who is distant. Nor is he a Father who withholds himself from us. We are members of his family, not his orphanage. He hears us. He answers us. Herein lies the seed from which this prophecy grows. Our Father is One who loves us and communes intimately with us. When we collectively, as his global church, get that revelation, we will step into the fullness of Isaiah's envisioned world. Until then, as individuals here and local churches there gain this revelation of who we are in Christ, successive enemies are placed under Christ's feet. And ultimately under our feet because we are in him.

> The wolf and the lamb shall feed together, the lion shall eat straw like the ox, and dust shall be the serpent's food. They shall not hurt nor destroy in all My holy mountain, says the Lord. (Isaiah 65:25)

I am happy if you want to spiritualize this image or take it word for word. Before the Fall, man was charged with having dominion over the earth. This was never intended to be expressed in an abusive discharge of power but was to reflect the kind of leadership that the Creator himself exercised. Not domineering but stewarding. As we march ever nearer the return of Christ, we will progressively step into our role as heavenly stewards of the creation. It will affect everything.

> And in that day, you will say: "O Lord, I will praise You; though You were angry with me, Your anger is

turned away, and You comfort me. Behold, God is my salvation, I will trust and not be afraid; for YAH, the LORD, is my strength and song; He also has become my salvation."

ISAIAH 12:1–2

Conclusion

I TRUST THAT AS you have worked your way through this book, you have picked up one essential message: God speaks to us about the future, not to tickle our ears or to hold out the prospect of things to come, but to change the way we live today. Do not be one who lives for tomorrow. Bring tomorrow into your today. The message of Christ's return is a message of Hope, not of Fear. It is a message that ultimately will show you who you are in Christ. It will open to you a surrounding world of possibilities as you step into your God-given identity. It will kill your allegiance to performance and fill you with faith in the all-pervading Grace of God.

Time to pray. Time to tell others. Time to belong. Time to be bold. Time to love. Time to step out in faith.

> Strengthen the weak hands, and make firm the feeble knees. Say to those who are fearful-hearted, "Be strong, do not fear! Behold, your God will come with vengeance, with the recompense of God; He will come and save you." Then the eyes of the blind shall be opened, and the ears of the deaf shall be unstopped. Then the lame shall leap like a deer, and the tongue of the dumb sing. For waters shall burst forth in the wilderness, and streams in the desert. The parched ground shall become a pool, and the thirsty land springs of water; in the habitation of

Conclusion

jackals, where each lay, there shall be grass with reeds and rushes. A highway shall be there, and a road, and it shall be called the Highway of Holiness. The unclean shall not pass over it, but it shall be for others. Whoever walks the road, although a fool, shall not go astray. No lion shall be there, nor shall any ravenous beast go up on it; it shall not be found there. But the redeemed shall walk there, and the ransomed of the Lord shall return, and come to Zion with singing, with everlasting joy on their heads. They shall obtain joy and gladness, and sorrow and sighing shall flee away.

Isaiah 35:3–10

Glossary

Apocalypse: a transliteration of the Greek word, *apokalupsis*, meaning *revelation*. The word is usually used to indicate the time of the end, just prior to the return of Christ. Apocalyptic writing is a genre of literature common at the time of Christ. It is marked by a heavy use of symbolism, numbers, colors, and cosmic upheavals.

Apostasy: the abandonment of religion. In the context of this book, I have treated apostasy as being, not the abandonment of religion in general, but the abandonment of true religion. An apostate church is one which is Christian in name but not in practice.

Canon: the official compilation of Old and/or New Testament books that are recognized as being the authoritative Word of God.

Dispensationalism: also called Dispensational Premillennialism, based on the belief that God deals with people in historical eras, or dispensations, in which different covenantal rules apply. Regarding the Second Coming, it is a Prophetic School of interpretation that teaches that eschatological prophecies find their fulfilment in a small period of time (typically seven years) immediately prior to Christ's visible return.

Eschatology: from the Greek *eschatos* meaning *last*. It is the theologians' term for the doctrine of the last things, that is, the doctrine of Christ's return.

GLOSSARY

Historical Premillennialism: the Prophetic School of interpretation that believes that prophecies relating to the Second Coming find progressive fulfilment over the timespan between the prophecy's first utterance and the return of Christ.

Idealism: the Prophetic School of interpretation that believes that prophecies concerning the Second Coming speak intentionally to every generation. Prophecy is seen to have a cyclic nature and may carry more than one fulfilment.

Millennium: from the Latin *mille*, meaning *thousand*, and *annus*, meaning *year*. It is the term used for the thousand year period in which Christ reigns, described in Revelation 20. Because this is a key point of divergence amongst the various schools of Eschatology, it attracts its own terminology amongst theologians. Amillennialism is the belief that Christ returns after a non-literal millennium that commenced with the conversion of believers, i.e. we have been in the millennium since Christ's ascension. Postmillennialism is the belief that Christ returns after the millennium, a period, either literal or not, that commences with the church effectively Christianizing the world as it steps into its true identity as the Beloved of the Lamb. Premillennialism is the belief that Jesus returns before the millennium, a thousand year period when Christ sets up his governmental rule based in Jerusalem in the Middle East, commencing with the resurrection of believers.

Preterism: the Prophetic School of interpretation that believes that all Biblical prophecy related specifically to the world and time of the prophet who wrote it and is therefore fulfilled already.

Recommended Reading

Chant, Barry, and W. Pratney. *The Return*. Sovereign World, 1991.
Chant, Ken. *When the Trumpet Sounds*. Vision, 2013.
Dunn, James. *Unity and Diversity in the New Testament*. SCM, 1990.
France, R. T. *Matthew, An Introduction and Survey*. Tyndale New Testament Commentaries. IVP Academic, 1985.
Hendricksen, William. *More than Conquerors*. Baker Book House, 1982.
Keil, Carl Friedrich, and Franz Delitzsch. *Commentary on the Old Testament*. Volumes 7, 9 & 10. Grand Rapids, 1975.
Minear, Paul. *I Saw a New Earth: An Introduction to the Visions of the Apocalypse*. Corpus Books, 1968.
Morris, Leon. *Revelation*. Tyndale New Testament Commentaries. IVP Academic, 1969.
Prevost, Jean-Pierre. *How to Read the Apocalypse*. SCM, 1993.

Subject Index

666—mark of the beast, 117–18, 125–27

antichrist, 128–30
Armageddon, 85–87

beast from the sea, 116–23

cashless society, 125–27

Daniel's 70 weeks, 143–50

Ezekiel's Temple, 135–38

false prophet, 124–27

Gog and Magog, 87–95
great apostacy, 138–39

Israel in Old Testament eschatology, 11–19

judgment day, 110–12

man of lawlessness, 130–35
millennium, 103–13

new heavens and new earth, 113, 150–54
new Jerusalem, 70–71

rapture, 43–44
rider on the white horse, 68–70

seven churches of Revelation, 51–55
signs of the times, 27

thief in the night, 101–2
time, times, and half a time, 140–43
tribulation, 73–77
two witnesses, 77–84

woman in the wilderness, 95–98

Scripture Index

to Prophecies discussed in this book

Isaiah

7:14—8:18	20–21
65:17–25	150–54

Ezekiel

38–39	87–90
40–48	135–38

Daniel

7:13–14	34–35
9:24–27	143–49

Hosea

1:2—2:23	15–17

Zechariah

3:1—4:14	79–81
12:1—14:21	90–95

Matthew

24–25	25–46

1 Corinthians

15:23–26	109–10

1 Thessalonians

5:1–9	101–2

2 Thessalonians

2:1–15	130–35

2 Timothy

3:1–5	138–39

2 Peter

3:3–13	112–14

Revelation

2–3	52–55
4:1—11:18	61–62
7:13–17	74–77
11:1–14	77–84
11:19—15:4	63–64
12:1–11	95–98
13:1–10	119–20, 122–23
13:11–17	124–27
13:16–18	116–18
15:5—19:10	64–66
16:12–16	85–87
17:3–14	121–22

Revelation (continued)

19:11—22:5	66–71
19:11–16	68–70
20:1–10	103–8
20:11–15	110–12

www.ingramcontent.com/pod-product-compliance
Lightning Source LLC
Chambersburg PA
CBHW072133160426
43197CB00012B/2095